M000200405

BROOKE SAWARD is a writer, a photographer, an explorer and a dreamer. She spends most of her days living out of a suitcase and, the few days of the year she's home, you'll find her on a farm in Tasmania. She is an advocate of a work–travel lifestyle and her only wish is to continue being adventurous, for as long as she lives.

worldofwanderlust.com

World of Wanderlust

how to live an adventurous life . . .

BROOKE SAWARD

VIKING
an imprint of
PENGUIN BOOKS

CONTENTS

THE BASICS

PLACES YOU MUST VISIT IN YOUR LIFETIME

SEE IT WITH YOUR OWN EYES

TRAVEL TIPS

HOW TO ESCAPE

(without actually going anywhere)

WANDERLUST DIRECTORY

INTRODUCTION

To everyone who has ever believed in a dream.

On the day of my graduation, I woke up feeling numb. I had finally come to the end of my education and I was sure I should have felt some kind of fulfilment. And yet I had never felt less like myself in my life.

With a sudden burst of courage, I reached for my laptop and typed a destination into a flight search engine. Within a matter of minutes I had done it: I had booked a one-way ticket to London.

I walked out of my room and declared I was leaving home in the New Year, giving myself a reasonable deadline to save enough money to last at least a year travelling the world. A few years later and I'm still going.

For as long as I can remember I have been restless. I have had the desire to escape the island I live on and venture to foreign lands. I long to experience new things: cities where no one knows my name, fields of sunflowers, boat rides along the Zambezi, searching for treasure in the Caribbean, jumping into waterfalls, diving out of planes, climbing mountains, riding horses . . . the list is truly endless. But as fate would have it, I did all of the above and more in just a year of travelling alone.

After only a few months, I realised I would be strapped for cash if I didn't start to make money somehow. Going home wasn't an option. It wasn't where my heart was. So I sold all my things, packed my bags and handed over my passport at immigration . . . never did I think I would return with all the pages filled!

I was avidly typing away each night on my blog, World of Wanderlust, which was my online journal of cities visited, people met and destinations conquered. As more and more people started reading it, I soon realised that this could become my full-time job. I wanted to create a space on the internet that others could escape to as well. A place where, no matter where you were in the world, you could always feel as though you were somewhere else, living vicariously through the experiences and photos I was sharing online.

During that year my passion became my purpose. I realised that travel not only brought me happiness in its truest form, but that travel could do the same for everyone who gave it a shot and hit the open road. So I started to spread the message quicker than you can spread raspberry jam on your toast.

The following pages are filled with ideas and inspiration for my fellow wanderers. We are young, wild and free (that's you, wild thing). We can't commit to a postcode, let alone a nine-to-five job. We want to learn, grow and evolve in the purest way possible – to adventure, explore, seek and find.

We're not lost and we don't want or need to be found. We are wanderers for the sake of wandering.

But adventure needn't be distant. Travel both near and far. If you have it in your bones, you'll make every day an adventure. When life throws you lemons, make lemonade.

Escape into my world of never-ending adventures.

Brooke Saward

Wanderlust

noun

a strong desire to travel

'a (wo)man consumed by wanderlust'

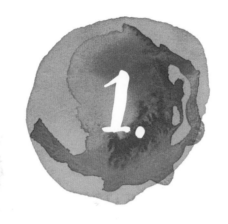

THE
BASICS

RULES TO LIVE (AND DIE) BY

I've never been one for following rules. I don't even let myself acknowledge them most of the time. So I'd rather think the following three mantras are guidelines to follow, not rules that are set in stone.

1. Wear Your Heart on Your Sleeve

(there's never enough love in this world)

2. Keep Your Feet on the Ground

(always stay humble)

3. Leave Your Head in the Clouds

(we are the dreamers)

Be respectful. We travel to see what is different in the world, but soon enough all we see are similarities.

Answer questions about your culture. Let the education run both ways. Others are just as interested in you as you are in them.

Keep your composure. Stay cool.

Be willing to learn. Travel is the best education.

Never stop exploring. Let the adventure live on.

10 TRAVEL COMMANDMENTS

Be independent. Read about your destination and research it, but be flexible with your itinerary. Don't be a guidebook warrior.

Keep an open mind. Remember it's not wrong, it's just different.

Take your time. Because wasting time is not time wasted.

Interact with the locals. You'll learn so much more about a country when you get to know its people.

Say YES to new things. Try new foods, make new friends, enjoy new experiences.

4

COMMON TRAVELLER TYPES

Ultra-enthusiastic

They start counting down more than 100 days out, have their bags packed at least a week before fly-out day, and are bouncing off the walls of an otherwise boring airport as they go to board their first flight. They're a great replacement for an alarm clock as they'll always be raring to go at first light, just don't travel with them for more than a couple of weeks or your eyes might be drooping towards your chin.

How to deal: wear them out by encouraging them to squeeze in a run (solo) before you meet them for breakfast each day.

Debbie downers

They probably never wanted to go on this trip and they'll let you know that on a daily basis. They're not excited about the Eiffel Tower because 'What is its function, anyway?' and they couldn't care less about the world's best ice-cream available in a quadzillion flavour combinations. The only thing they're excited about is home time and, until then, you've gotta spend a double dose of energy trying to pull them through the trip.

How to deal: run away, pronto. You picked the wrong travel buddy.

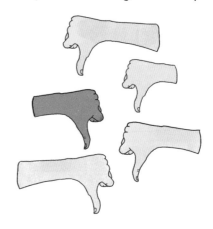

Uneducated and unconcerned

Perhaps my favourite kind of traveller – until day two. It all starts out as a bit of a novelty as you find yourself explaining the history, culture, architecture and other relevant facts of a new city to your uneducated and unconcerned counterpart. Then by day two you're tired of answering questions and acting like a tour guide.

How to deal: buy them a relevant city guide before your trip and ensure they read it on the plane.

Full nomad

You can spot a full nomad a mile away, looking enviously chilled out, laid back, maybe even with a cockatoo on their shoulder. They prefer bare feet, salt in their hair and sun-soaked skin.

How to deal: let yourself fall under the nomadic spell! Some of your best travel memories will be made barefoot, salty-haired and carefree.

Ultra-organised

The ultra-organised traveller has cut down a forest in order to print all the printables prior to your trip. This kind of traveller is great if you're not interested in doing any of the planning, but if you have any specific interests that vary from theirs, don't expect them to be catered for.

How to deal: encourage spontaneity and, in the worst case, be prepared to make a run for it!

History buff
(aka the know-it-all)

On the other side of the scale you have the know-it-alls, who just so happen to know it all (even when they don't). They're eager to play tour guide and tell anyone who will listen how much they know, so be sure to pack some headphones for when you're ready to tune out (zzz).

How to deal: if the headphones don't go over well, claim you read differently in a guidebook on the way over and get them to doubt their knowledge . . . even if it's just for kicks.

The reminiscer

The reminiscer is a great travel buddy while abroad and even greater when you return home. They're the ones who remember all the fine details, from the name of those delicious Portugese tarts to what happened after you drank straight vodka in Russia to prove to the bar tender that foreigners aren't any weaker than locals.

How to deal: you have no worries here! Come one, come all!

Bad-arse budgeter

These guys know their stuff. They've spent hours, days, weeks, even, researching how to save a buck. They know the discount days, they keep a daily logbook of how much they've spent, and they'll be the last person to splurge on an experience not already factored into their budget.

How to deal: don't get too caught up in money matters while abroad, make your trip count!

High-fliers

The high-fliers seem to have it all . . . they know all the ins and outs of frequent flyer programs and can swing an upgrade with the fluttering of eyelids.

How to deal: befriend a high-flier on the plane or in the airport and you'll score free access to the business lounge. Oh yeah!

THE NEW COMMON

The digital nomad

Once upon a time, travel was a luxury reserved for the elite. Nowadays, this truth has thankfully been turned on its head.

Wondering how so many people travel for more days of the year than they spend at home?

Introducing the **digital nomad**.

It is now more than ever entirely possible to travel more, travel longer, and to travel and work as a digital nomad. One can be or do almost anything without qualifications. Why? Because the internet exists. You're just one quick search away from learning everything you need to know about becoming a social media consultant, a digital analyst, a remote marketer, or learning how to code, filming your own videos, writing your own ebooks, and more.

Get creative, learn a new skill, make a plan to work online while you travel and you're good to go.

COMMON TRIPS TO TAKE

The gap year

A gap year is often seen as a chance to get out there and see the world while you're young, fit and able, before coming home to settle into university studies and eventually a career. But be warned! Not all gap year-goers come back after seeing so much opportunity abroad (not that this is at all a bad thing). Should you feel said desire to stay away, don't be afraid to extend your trip and stay a little longer! Often gap year-goers take up opportunities that arise abroad for a more exciting line of work – many try yachting, bartending, becoming an au pair, etc.

Mid-twenties crisis

This trip is most common among those who didn't take a gap year, and who saw everyone else around them out there exploring the world, having a great time and creating a new life for themselves. All the while these prone-to-crisis twenty-somethings are stuck moving paper from one side of their desk to the other. They yearn for an office with a window, just so they can have some sort of connection to the outside world. Then all of a sudden they break, usually triggered by a flight sale for Europe, and off they go. Really, this is almost inevitable.

Pre-settle-down splurge

This is also known as the 'last hurrah' trip, taken by those with their lives pretty well sorted out. They are so good at planning that they know years in advance when a baby will be on the way, so they make it their very last trip of freedom – no curfews, no limits, no budgets . . . no cares! But settling down needn't be confined to babies and walking down the aisle, a pre-settle-down splurge can also offer freedom before settling into a long life of dreaded mortgage repayments. If you don't go now, when will be your next chance?

Spend the kids' inheritance

Another trip I entirely condone is a parent's decision to spend their later years in style. After spending your life working hard to make a living, what excuse do you have not to go? Parents deserve every chance they can get to be a kid again, so be sure to encourage them along before it's too late. And so what if they've packed a bumbag and a visor? Style takes many forms.

Mid-life crisis

This trip really needs no explanation. It can occur anytime in your forties or fifties and often coincides with a decision to purchase a Harley motorbike. If you know someone approaching a mid-life crisis or are entering one yourself, remember, you've earned it. You've made it halfway, it's time to let your hair down.

Wanderlust Playlist

Mumford & Sons	*Hopeless Wanderer*
Red Hot Chili Peppers	*Road Trippin'*
The Kooks	*Seaside*
Angus & Julia Stone	*Big Jet Plane*
Sufjan Stevens	*Chicago*
Frank Turner	*Wanderlust*
Joseph Arthur	*Honey and the Moon*
City and Colour	*Comin' Home*
The Kooks	*See the World*
Death Cab for Cutie	*Soul Meets Body*
Frank Turner	*Sunshine State*
Angus & Julia Stone	*Santa Monica Dream*
Bag Raiders	*Way Back Home*
Gypsy & the Cat	*Time to Wander*
Dido	*Life for Rent*
Wildlife	*Hotel California*
Vampire Weekend	*Holiday*
Noah and the Whale	*5 Years Time*

Adventure Travel

Some of the best adventures are to be had camping in your own backyard, in the passenger seat on a full-day road trip, or facing your fears rock climbing in the national park nearest to your home. Adventure travel doesn't require you go far or be anywhere in particular, but just for you to be there and be present, wherever you are. For those times you want to live and not just exist, here's a round-up of the best adventure experiences both near and far.

CAGE DIVING

Skydiving

Microflight

CAMEL RIDING

TOP TEN ADVENTURE
ACTIVITIES
AROUND THE WORLD

*Dune
Bashing*

Tubing

*Helicopter
Flight*

BUNGY JUMPING

Paragliding

ZIP LINING

GRAB YOUR FRIENDS, WE'RE GOING CAMPING

Aim: go on a camping trip reminiscent of your childhood days.

RULES
(should you choose to accept them):

- No screens (phones, laptops, Nintendo 64s are out)
- No cooking appliances, outside of sticks for your sausages and marshmallows
- In fact, let's just say no modern appliances or technology at all
- Plenty of fun
- Plenty of laughs
- A campfire is a necessity
- Tents must be assembled by all attendees
- Source water from a running stream, y'know, like the old days

YOU'LL NEED:

- Instant camera
- Pen and paper
- Guitar for campfire serenades (ukulele substitute more than okay)
- Cringe-worthy camp food
- Sleeping bags
- Tent
- Spotlight
- Multi-purpose knife (caveman style)

UNSAID RULES OF A ROAD TRIP

- Shotgun can only be called within eyesight of the vehicle.

- The tallest and/or largest person belongs in the front seat, overriding any and all claims if they are distinctly taller or larger than the person calling shotgun.

- All passengers should pitch in money for petrol, no IOUs accepted.

- Pit stops aren't an option but a necessity – it's the journey that matters in the end!

- The front-seat passenger is in charge of the music. However, the driver can request an unlimited number of song changes.

- No passenger has the right to criticise the car owner's tidiness (unless it is impacting on their reasonable amount of legroom).

- In a full car, the horrid and unforgiving middle seat belongs to the smallest and/or shortest passenger.

- The navigator must be able to read a road map and give clear directions to the driver.

- Should the navigator be incapable of performing aforementioned responsibilities, the navigator will be stripped of their title (and front seat), forcing a new navigator to present themselves.

- The driver has the final say on air temperature, pit stops, and just generally gets to play boss from start to finish. Should the driver abuse their privileges, passengers may rally for a dethroning.

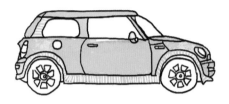

Road Trip Playlist

Willie Nelson	*On the Road Again*
Lynyrd Skynyrd	*Sweet Home Alabama*
Steppenwolf	*Born to be Wild*
The Rolling Stones	*Route 66*
Tom Cochrane	*Life is a Highway*
Ray Charles	*Hit the Road Jack*
U2	*Where the Streets Have No Name*
Bruce Springsteen	*Born to Run*
Flock of Seagulls	*I Ran (So Far Away)*
Edward Sharpe and the Magnetic Zeros	*Home*

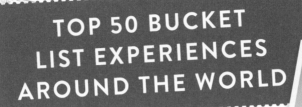

TOP 50 BUCKET LIST EXPERIENCES AROUND THE WORLD

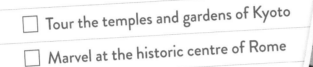

- [ ] Tour the temples and gardens of Kyoto
- [ ] Marvel at the historic centre of Rome
- [ ] See the Serengeti migration
- [ ] Get soaked by Iguazu Falls
- [ ] Journey to Machu Picchu
- [ ] Dip into the Blue Lagoon in Iceland
- [ ] Float in the Dead Sea
- [ ] Spin 360° at Times Square
- [ ] Visit the holy land of Jerusalem
- [ ] See London from a double-decker bus

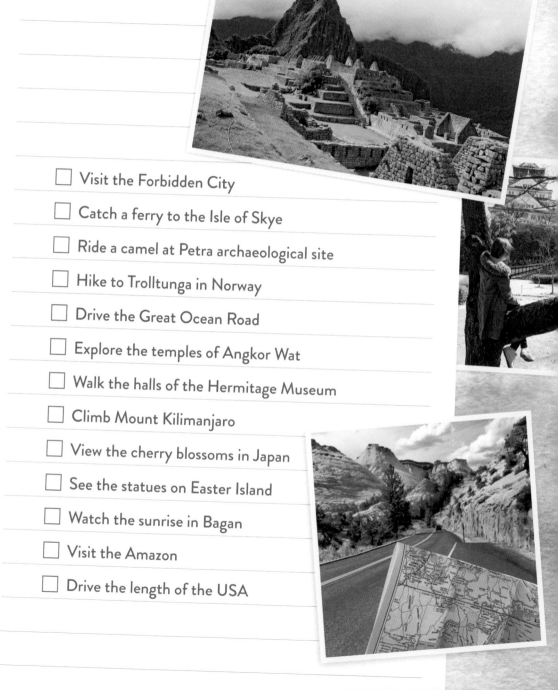

- [ ] Visit the Forbidden City
- [ ] Catch a ferry to the Isle of Skye
- [ ] Ride a camel at Petra archaeological site
- [ ] Hike to Trolltunga in Norway
- [ ] Drive the Great Ocean Road
- [ ] Explore the temples of Angkor Wat
- [ ] Walk the halls of the Hermitage Museum
- [ ] Climb Mount Kilimanjaro
- [ ] View the cherry blossoms in Japan
- [ ] See the statues on Easter Island
- [ ] Watch the sunrise in Bagan
- [ ] Visit the Amazon
- [ ] Drive the length of the USA

- [ ] Jump off the old bridge in Mostar, Bosnia and Herzegovina
- [ ] Step foot on Antarctica
- [ ] See New England in the fall
- [ ] See the northern lights
- [ ] Row a boat in Lake Bled
- [ ] Stroll through the gardens of the Palace of Versailles
- [ ] Drink beer at the famous Oktoberfest
- [ ] Feel small below the Christ the Redeemer statue in Rio de Janeiro
- [ ] See the pyramids of Giza
- [ ] View the Taj Mahal at first light
- [ ] Eat gelato in Italy
- [ ] Wander through Istanbul's Grand Bazaar
- [ ] See the Pantanal
- [ ] Walk along the Great Wall of China
- [ ] Wander through Plitvice Lakes National Park

- [ ] Get lost in a lantern daze in Hoi An
- [ ] Go trekking in the Himalayas
- [ ] Ride in a hot air balloon in Cappadocia
- [ ] Dive into the Great Barrier Reef
- [ ] Step inside a time warp in Old Havana
- [ ] View the Grand Canyon
- [ ] Spot wildlife in the Canadian Rockies
- [ ] Sing to *The Sound of Music* in Salzburg
- [ ] Hike in Patagonia
- [ ] See an opera performance at the Vienna State Opera House
- [ ] Dodge the snake charmers in the medina of Marrakech
- [ ] View Uluru

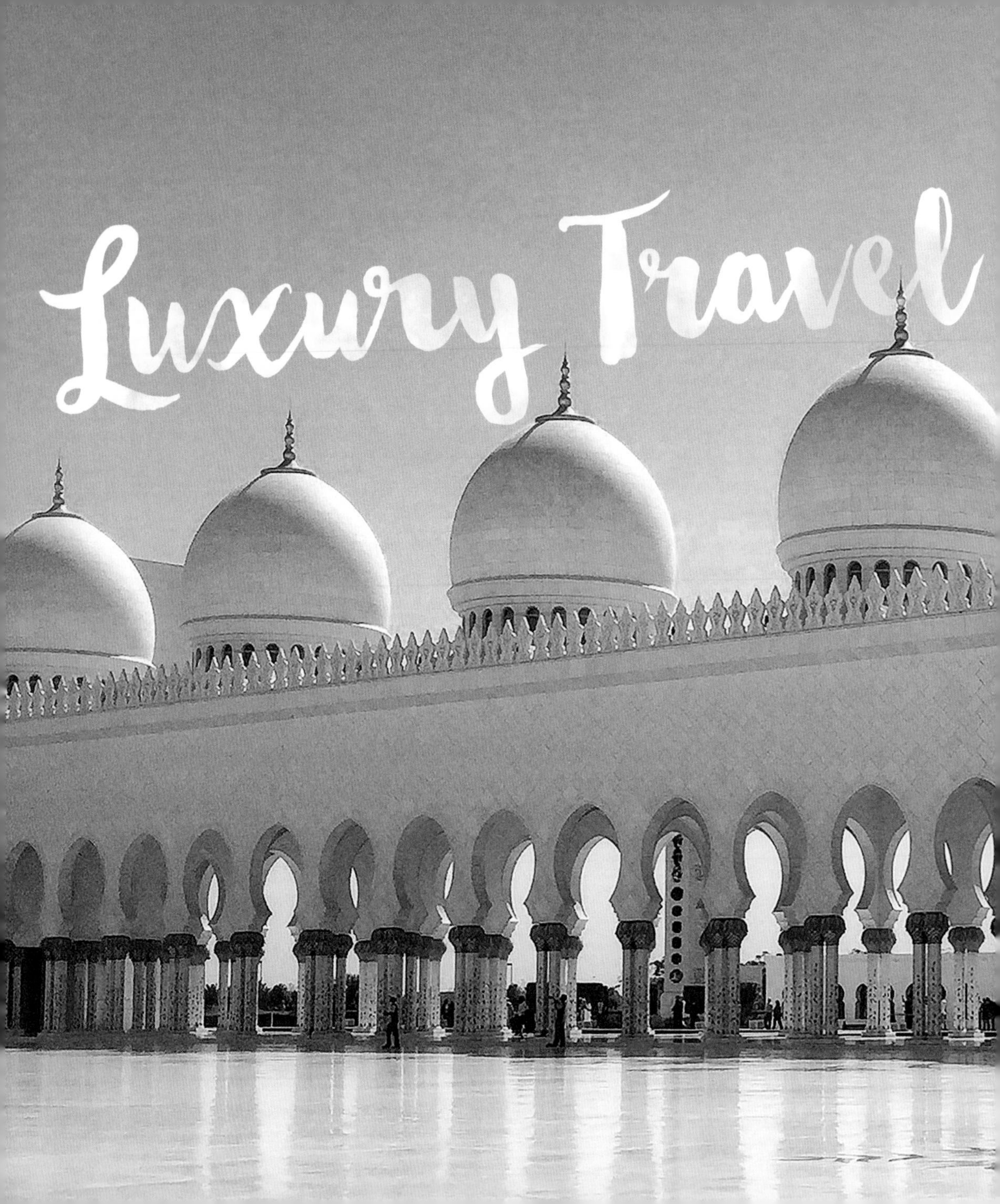
Luxury Travel

THE BEST SPA TREATMENTS
AROUND THE WORLD

Dead Sea Mud Wrap

Many travellers make their way to the
Dead Sea to bathe in its extremely
salty waters and experience the
sensation of floating, but many also
come purely for the Dead Sea mud!
Cover yourself in a combination
of minerals and kick back in the
water to feel completely relaxed
and rejuvenated and you'll walk
away with soft, silky skin.

Finnish Sauna

It will be hard to ever forget my
introduction to Finnish saunas, having run
barefoot from the sauna to the icy lake
to fully immerse myself, head to toe,
in freezing-cold water. In winter the lakes
freeze over and the Fins, being the Fins
(they can't go without their sauna), cut a
small hole into the ice for a post-sauna dip.

Thermal Spas and Hot Springs

The craze of thermal spas and hot
springs has taken off over the years,
especially since the Blue Lagoon
just outside of Reykjavik, Iceland,
opened its doors to visitors. Thermal
spas and springs offer your body
complete relaxation in hot water
that is derived from the earth's
crust. They are hugely popular
all over the world!

Turkish Hammam

Very different from the traditional roman bathing rituals, the Turkish hammam focuses on water instead of steam. This is one travel experience you will want to splurge on as the more you pay, the better the spa facilities and the more enjoyable the treatment will be! You'll go through a process of a warm room, a hot room, a full cleanse and massage, finished with a cooling room or dip in cold water to get the blood pumping. Although it comes as quite a shock to the body, the Turkish hammam is recognised as one of the most cleansing spa treatments in the world!

Roman Baths

Roman bathing rituals have spread far and wide throughout the world, allowing you many opportunities to experience the traditional way of bathing. Typically you make a day out of it, moving from one hot room to the next: saunas, steam rooms, you name it. This is a great way to spend a slow Sunday (and a great way to transport yourself to another time and place with a little imagination!).

LUXURY HOTELS

Sometimes you just feel the need to splurge. Sure, you can't do that every day of every trip or before too long you won't be able to afford to go anywhere at all. But for the times when you really just want to (over) indulge, here are some of the world's most incredible hotels, all tried and tested to make sure that they really are as fabulous as the website photographs would have you believe.

Singita Sweni Lodge, South Africa

I'm woken by the sound of hippos beneath my treehouse dwelling, then I walk amongst giraffes to reach the restaurant where a three-course meal is provided thrice daily. Tours depart twice a day to photograph lions, zebras, hyenas and more, while professional trackers proudly share the unprecedented beauty of the Kruger National Park with guests. South Africa steals your heart and I left mine at Singita Sweni.

Nihiwatu Resort, Indonesia

Waking up to the sound of waves crashing, having breakfast with sand beneath your feet, a spa safari on the cliffs overlooking the Indian Ocean . . . there really isn't another place quite as idyllic and serene as Nihiwatu on Sumba Island.

The Pierre, a Taj Hotel, NYC, USA

There's no place in the world like this city: it's a world in itself. Perched twenty-something floors high above Central Park, I can't help but imagine this is my real life . . . The Pierre is as classic as they come, with elevator operators who are there to press the buttons for you and wish you a pleasant day . . . fancy, huh!

Salto Chico Hotel, Chile

There are hardly any views in the world that can compare to Torres del Paine – an adventure seeker's true paradise. Waking up each morning seeing this view with Lake Pehoe in the foreground is about as special as room views go. The experience includes all meals and guided walks daily, so there's not a worry in the world at Salto Chico!

The Ritz-Carlton, Hong Kong

High above the clouds is The Ritz-Carlton hotel, overlooking the city of Hong Kong. When it opened back in 2011, it was the tallest hotel in the world, with all hotel rooms being at least 102 floors high, peaking with Ozone bar on the 118th floor.

Solo Travel

HOW TO ENJOY SOLO TRAVEL

Solo travel isn't easy. There are the long train journeys, trying to squeeze yourself and your suitcase into an airport toilet cubicle and the unashamedly shameful 'dinner for one, please.'

Though they do say nothing worth doing comes easy!

Solo travel is challenging, but challenges bring rewards. And I can assure you, there is nothing more rewarding in life than learning to love time on your own, listening to your thoughts and manifesting ideas you never thought you were capable of. Travelling the world is undeniably the best education you can give yourself, and the opportunities once you hit the road are endless.

To enjoy solo travel, you just have to remember a few things.

Say YES to things you wouldn't normally do.

The most important thing to do when travelling solo is to keep busy and the best way to keep yourself busy is to try new things! This will not only lead to conquering your fears, but will also give you great stories to take home. Step outside your comfort zone, try new things, say YES.

Introduce yourself to strangers.

Some of the most interesting people
I have met have been in the most
random locations (right now I'm thinking
of the guy I met at the laundromat in
Berlin – so strangely wonderful). But if
you don't spark up a conversation and be
friendly to people, how can you expect
them to be friendly back? Be brave,
be bold, smile and talk to people.

Fill your music library and take time for yourself.

Sometimes you just don't want to listen or talk to
anyone . . . not even yourself. Before you depart
on your trip, be sure to fill your music library
with different tunes for different moods – slow
acoustic for the long train journeys, crazy beats
for those morning runs, fun upbeat pop for those
times you need to shake a bad mood.

Be open but mindful.

It's one thing to say 'go out
there and try everything offered
to you' when there's a lot that
could go wrong! It's important
to be realistic and safe.

Carpe diem.

Use every second of daylight for adventure and
take the evenings to update the world on your
whereabouts, or follow news and events. Stay in the
moment wherever possible (it is always possible).

HOW TO MAKE FRIENDS
WHEN YOU TRAVEL SOLO

As a self-confessed on/off introvert, one of the biggest fears I had before my first solo adventure was not being able to meet others. Around my friends and family I am a bubbly twenty-something who is full of life and conversation, and always ready for a laugh. However, around strangers, I seem to have this tortoise shell I retreat back inside to shield myself from the world around me.

And then I started travelling solo.

Over the years I have become a complete extrovert and am now more than happy to strike up a conversation with a stranger in the plane seat next to me. So how did I go from tortoise to 'Hi! I'm Brooke'?

Solo travel has a funny way of forcing you out of your comfort zone and into the depths of the unknown quite quickly.

Accommodation

I found that one of the easiest ways to make new friends with both travellers and locals was to book accommodation that requires being social. Hostels are an obvious choice, but if hostels aren't your thing (they're not for everyone!), then consider renting an apartment or a room in someone's home, as this is a great way to meet locals and allow them to give you insider recommendations, tips and advice. Plus you have someone to talk to at the end of each day.

In Transit

It should come as no surprise that one of the easiest ways to meet people is during the act of travelling itself. Whether you're on a plane, train or bus, be sure to strike up a conversation with the person next to you to see where they're going, where they're from, and where their favourite place in the world is (I've been given a great many secret locations this way!)

Group Tours

Just because you're travelling on your own does not mean you can't meet up with other travellers and have someone to enjoy things with! Group tours are a great option as they will give you a chance to break up the time on your own and to meet fellow travellers from all corners of the globe. It could be a multi-day trip or just the simple act of joining a day tour around a city. More often than not you'll meet one or two people who you'll stay in touch with or perhaps even meet elsewhere on your travels!

Start a Blog

When I started blogging about my travels online, I had no idea it would turn into an online community of hundreds of thousands of readers. After persisting with it over the course of a few months, I soon found myself being contacted by readers from different countries around the world, offering to show me around their city. All of a sudden I had the best of both worlds: travelling solo, which I love, but with someone to share it with. Better yet, I suddenly had thousands of new friends around the world!

THE BEST PLACES FOR SOLO TRAVEL

Choosing the best destinations in the world for solo travel is a pretty big ask, so let's break this down a little. Personally, I have always had the most enjoyable solo travel experiences when travelling in Europe. I think this is due to a number of factors: this region is very popular with people in my age group so that it is always easy to meet fellow travellers; the train network in Europe is seamless, affordable and even enjoyable; and because I'm a self-confessed history buff – and Europe has a lot of history. North America is easy enough to travel around solo and have a really great trip. However, hostels and accommodation for singles aren't nearly as popular as they are in Europe, so it can be a little more expensive when you're not splitting the costs! Asia is another great option for travel solo, but the culture shock may leave you feeling a little bit out of your depth and the last thing you want is to miss home when you're on the other side of the world. Then there is Africa and the Middle East, both great regions to explore and entirely possible to explore solo. Do be sure to research safety concerns prior to your trip as each country can differ substantially from the next. Whatever you choose, the following are my top picks for the best solo travel destinations around the world.

Europe

Europe has ample options for solo travellers, with the most popular being an all-encompassing 'Euro trip' around several countries, often in a short space of time. However, if you do wish to experience slow travel and get to know a particular country better, Ireland, Scotland, France, Belgium, Iceland and Finland are all great options. Each of these countries are known for their mesmerising landscapes and charming towns, and all of them are safe and comfortable to travel through on your own. Scotland and Ireland are great choices for extroverted travellers who like to meet and spend time with locals – it's hard to find a Scotsman or Irishman not willing to strike up a conversation! The French, Belgians and Finnish are a little more reserved as a whole, making these great destinations for people who prefer to keep to themselves or enjoy time in solitude.

Asia

Fancy your very own *Eat Pray Love* moment in spiritual Bali? Or is the hustle and bustle of Bangkok more your style? Whether you're after tranquillity or turmoil, you'll surely find it in Asia. I'd recommend focusing on Southeast Asia as it has really become a hub for solo travellers over the years. Thailand is a great place to start. If you're looking to meet fellow travellers, there are a great range of companies offering group treks and trips through Cambodia and Laos that are cheap, safe and have ever-improving transportation connections. Vietnam is another popular choice, thanks to its people, culture, history and incredible cuisine. And it is still one of the cheaper options in the region.

Travellers with more to spend and who are interested in broadening their scope might consider Japan, Malaysia, Singapore and Taiwan. All of these countries are incredibly safe, though they will require a substantially bigger budget.

Middle East

In the media, the Middle East is often depicted as an unsafe region to travel to, particularly for solo travellers. This is mostly untrue, with a few obvious exceptions. While Middle Eastern countries do share similarities, each is entirely different in its own right. Countries suited to solo travellers that are safer to travel to include the United Arab Emirates and Jordan. More recently Oman and Qatar have opened themselves to tourism, too. The United Arab Emirates includes the popular cities of Abu Dhabi and Dubai, each of which appear Western on the surface but operate under strict local laws and customs, specifically regarding public affection and alcohol. Jordan has had a steady increase in tourism due to the iconic site of Petra, while Qatar and Oman offer very authentic experiences a little off the beaten path. To ensure your safety, be sure to stay updated with news and events in the country you plan to visit.

Africa

South Africa is a great choice if you want to experience the quintessential 'trip to Africa' without too much to worry about. There won't be any extra flights throughout the continent and, for a large number of passport holders, visas are not required for stays of up to ninety days. English is widely spoken in South Africa and it is one of the best countries to visit on the continent. It really has it all – wildlife safaris, a gorgeous coastline with ample marine-life watching, the iconic city of Cape Town, and so much history to soak up that you'll leave with a better understanding of not just South Africa but the African continent as a whole. Alternatively, if you're looking to experience a once-in-a-lifetime trip to the Sahara desert, find your way through a maze of souks, sip on mint tea or experience a traditional hammam, then Morocco is a great choice in North Africa, and just a short flight from many European cities.

South America

For adventurous travellers who are looking for experiences unlike anywhere else in the world, there really is so much on offer in South America. From Iguazu Falls on the border of Brazil, Paraguay and Argentina, to Christ the Redeemer in Rio de Janeiro, to the salt flats of Bolivia, South America is full of bucket list destinations, experiences and sights to see. The best countries for solo travellers are those that have lots to offer to keep you entertained, as well as being safer options frequented by other travellers. Great choices include Brazil, Argentina and Chile. If joining a group tour, other options include heading further north to Peru and Ecuador.

Oceania

Australia is an absolute favourite for solo travellers who are looking to go off the grid, explore a vast nation with plenty to offer, and return home to the jealousy of their friends. For most people around the world, Australia is a dream destination but, due to its remote geographic location, many travellers only visit if they can afford a longer period of time away. From the outback to the Great Barrier Reef, Australia has a lot to offer the adventurous type.

Its smaller but equally charming neighbour New Zealand is another popular choice. Both New Zealand and Australia are extremely safe and, as a lot of solo travellers choose to visit, there are plenty of opportunities to meet others along the way. While in the area, be sure to consider other locations in the Pacific such as Fiji, Samoa, Tonga . . . the list goes on. Oceania is full of island life, so be sure to allow yourself plenty of time to soak up the sunshine and experience the culture of the Pacific.

North and Central America

If you're looking for diversity in abundance, national parks, incredible coastlines and colourful cities, then you should consider North America for a grand solo adventure. Many travellers visit the USA on a whirlwind trip, hopping from city to city, and manage to convince themselves they've seen it all because they've collected city names such as New York, Los Angeles, San Francisco, Washington DC and Boston. But this couldn't be further from the truth. These cities are excellent and must be visited at least once in your lifetime, but until you go beyond the coastlines and into the heart of the USA, you can't really say you've done it at all! Be bold and brave and take a slow pace.

Highlights include: Arizona, a state that has so much natural beauty you'll be baffled as to why Americans don't spend more time in their backyard; California, which, while an obvious choice, has so many amazing sights when travelling from north to south along the Pacific Coast Highway; the Rockies, if you're after a winter wonderland adventure; and of course you can't go past the Deep South. North and South Carolina, Georgia, Tennessee and Texas are all standouts.

For the really adventurous travellers who wish to spend all or most of their time outdoors, there are outstanding national parks to visit further north. Try venturing into Canada. Some exceptional provinces for solo explorers include Alberta, British Columbia, Nova Scotia, Newfoundland and Labrador. Still haven't had enough? Mexico and the Caribbean have always been well-liked holiday destinations for North Americans. However, in recent years it has become increasingly popular to venture into the depths of the Costa Rican jungle or the beautiful blue waters of Nicaragua. While these countries are slightly more expensive than others in the area due to the recent influx of travellers, they are among some of the safest countries in the region and certainly have some of the most incredible scenery, culture and wildlife.

Solo Travel Films

Into the Wild
(2007)

Eat Pray Love
(2010)

Tracks
(2013)

Wild
(2014)

The Motorcycle Diaries
(2004)

The Secret Life of Walter Mitty
(2013)

One Week
(2008)

L'Auberge Espagnole
(2002)

The Beach
(1999)

The Art of Travel
(2008)

HOW TO TAKE SOLO TRAVEL PHOTOS

YOU'LL NEED:

- A camera
- A flexible tripod
- Patience

Hey presto!

HOW TO CONVINCE SOMEONE TO TRAVEL WITH YOU

You want to travel but you don't want to go it alone. You've thrown the idea around with a bunch of friends and no one has taken the bait . . . now what?

Before finding the desire and the courage to travel solo, I found myself facing this exact dilemma. I wanted to go on a short trip at the end of each year, even if it was just to a country nearby (which for me, being an Australian, is usually pretty exotic by my standards).

After so many lost opportunities for dirt-cheap airline tickets, hotel offers popping up in my inbox or festivals coming and going, I decided I needed to up my game and learn how to convince someone to travel with me. Here's what I came up with:

1. Different minds are inspired by different things

Photos, videos, online articles and blog posts: there are different triggers for different individuals. For me, being a visual person, I am often inspired to go somewhere after seeing an incredible photo or article showcasing a destination. However, it is always different depending on the person. Many people have a case of FOMO (fear of missing out), which you can totally use to your advantage.

2. Offer to cover some of the expenses

There were times when I got so desperate that I did the math and realised that going alone would cost me nearly as much as if I were two people, disregarding the airfares. So I made an offer to my friend that I would cover the cost of the hotel and all they'd need to pay would be their airfare.

3. Do the hard work for them

Coming to someone with an idea is one thing, but coming to them with a detailed plan is a totally different ball game. By outlining the itinerary and all the fun you will have, your potential travel companion is likely to see what they'll be missing out on if they don't tag along. You can also outline things like daily expenses to convince them that travel doesn't have to be as expensive as they believe it to be!

4. Make them an offer that is too good to refuse

It was the end of my second year at university when I phoned my mum after my last exam and said, 'Mum, we're going to Thailand!' I had found a two-for-one flight deal that meant I could cover both my flight and hers for just the price of my own. We then split the accommodation costs and both benefited from the deal.

5. Reconsider going alone

In some cases, it just isn't possible to convince anyone to travel with you. Whether they have work or family commitments or just don't wish to travel, there are times when, no matter how convincing you are, no one will want to come on your trip. I reached this point after a few years of convincing family members and friends to travel with me and finally decided that it was as good a time as any to start travelling solo. I was nervous, unprepared and entirely unsure of my decision but, as is usually the case with anything new you try, once the first trip was out of the way it was smooth sailing.

HOW TO STAY SANE WHEN TRAVELLING WITH FRIENDS

The flights were booked, the hotel was reserved, my bags were packed and I was walking out of my Berlin apartment to meet my best friend from Australia to travel to Paris for the weekend together.

While I love spending time with my friends and more specifically travelling with them, I had spent nearly the entire year beforehand travelling alone. I had been spoiled by the luxury of choosing when I woke up and when I fell asleep, as well as having no one over my shoulder to say I shouldn't eat three croissants at the breakfast buffet (and, in my humble opinion, I don't believe one can ever have too many croissants).

The effects of travelling with others started to hit me straight away: I was happy to catch the bus into the city while he insisted we catch a cab; I wanted to eat cheese and biscuits for lunch on-the-go while he wanted to sit down for a three-course meal; I wanted to walk the streets of Paris at night while he wanted to club-hop his way around the city from one nightspot to the next . . . and so on.

So, what did I learn?

Be flexible and take
an interest in the
things they would like
to do . . . who knows,
you might find a new
hobby yourself!

Finish each day
together to reflect
on your adventures
over dinner.

Compromise
or spend time
apart.

Be honest about the things
you really want to do.

Book twin beds or
two bedrooms if
you can.

Laugh it off – if you
have an argument,
take the high road
and remember
tomorrow is a
brand-new day.

Remember why they're your
friends and why you love them.
Overlook the trivialities of a
holiday and remember to make
memories to last a lifetime, not
those you'll wish to forget.

HOW TO TRAVEL WITH PARENTS
(And Actually Enjoy It)

Trust me . . . it can be done.

I haven't always loved travelling with my parents, but they have always been the most reliable travel companions. There's no one more enthusiastic about a trip away than parents, who are most probably still trying to digest the idea that their child *actually wants* to spend a designated amount of time with them. They'll never cancel at the last minute, they'll make a constant effort to prove themselves 'young and hip' – meaning they'll be enthusiastic about most activities – and they're a good last resort if your travel funds are running dry (wink).

Tips for Surviving the Parentals Overseas

- Go somewhere that neither you nor they have been.

- Find out what they're interested in doing *before* you depart for your trip so there's no disappointment on arrival.

- Encourage them to try new things but understand when 'No' is the only answer you'll get.

- Cater to their interests – who knows, you might just learn something from that random museum that you haven't heard about or read about in any of the guidebooks.

- Wake up early and seize the day.

- Make memories to last a lifetime.

'Travelling with Others' Films

Lost in Translation
(2003)

Monte Carlo
(2011)

The Bucket List
(2007)

EuroTrip
(2004)

Little Miss Sunshine
(2006)

The Best Exotic Marigold Hotel
(2011)

Vicky Christina Barcelona
(2008)

National Lampoon's Vacation
(1983)

Chasing Liberty
(2004)

Expatriate

noun

a person who lives outside
their native country

Living Abroad

QUESTIONS TO ASK YOURSELF BEFORE TRYING EXPAT LIFE

As a self-confessed travel addict, I have always been drawn to the idea of living abroad. 'But why?' my friends and family would ask me. 'Why not?' I would respond. For those of us who have the urge to live abroad, to experience a different culture, to learn a new language, to make new friends and to remove ourselves from everything we know about life back at home, the urge turns into reality eventually. But before you throw yourself into the deep end and make the move to a foreign country, here are a few questions to ask yourself (not others, you are your best voice of reason!).

My stomach was in knots when I finally decided that yes, I would rent an apartment in Berlin and have a home base in Europe for an undetermined amount of time. But it wasn't jitters or nerves that I was feeling; instead, I was excited by the idea. Be sure to distinguish how you feel about your move and channel that energy into your new home city: you really need to feel excited by the idea to enjoy it and make the most of your time living abroad.

Can I afford it?

Instead of skimping by on what money you have left at the end of your work week once you've paid the rent and bills, determine whether you can afford living life the way you like to live it at home. If you like eating out once or twice a week but won't be able to afford it in your new city, perhaps you won't enjoy living abroad at this point in your life. You need to ask yourself what is important to you and be sure not to sacrifice everything you enjoy in order to move. Move when the time is right for you and your finances.

Do I know anyone who lives there?

For different people this means different things. Some potential expats will be excited by the idea of moving to a new city where no one knows their name or their past. Others would prefer to move to a new city only if they know at least one person there, so the socialisation process is easier and there's always someone to call when things go wrong. It isn't hard to make friends once you're living abroad, however, do ask yourself this question and determine how you feel about the answer before jumping into the deep end.

What is the job market like?

If you don't have a job ready to go in your new city, be sure to do your homework beforehand. Research not only what the job market is like, but also what it is like for foreigners. Are they likely to hire you as an expat? Do you have the required qualifications? Are there jobs available in your field? Are you able to obtain a working visa in your new country and what are the obstacles in doing so? These are all necessary considerations before booking the one-way ticket.

What is the transport system like?

While this may not seem like a huge consideration at first, before you know it this will have a huge impact on your daily life. Be sure to research how effective and affordable the public transport system is in your new city so you know in advance how you will get around. This should also be a factor when choosing your neighbourhood to ensure you don't wind up with an absurdly long commute to work each day.

What are my expectations?

Finally, ask yourself why you want to move, what you expect to gain from the move, and whether you believe you will find these things in your chosen city. Often it is as simple as having a sudden urge to move overseas and start afresh, but in order to actually make the most of that change and enjoy your time as an expat, it is important to think about what you want and which city is right for you based on that. List your expectations and hang onto that piece of paper. A few months into your move, look back over the list and pause to reflect.

Eagerness to learn
You embrace the unknown and challenge yourself with it.

Will be the first person to recommend expat life
Because nothing feels better than sharing the thing that changed you with someone else who wants a change.

Open to seeing, doing and trying new things
You tire of the old and mundane; routine is not your forte. You embrace everything new around you.

Not afraid of a challenge
Everything is worth a try.

Happy-go-lucky
Cheerful about all things.

CHARACTERISTICS OF AN EXPAT

Glass half full
Optimism is your ideal.

Generally likes (all kinds of) food
Because food fixes any problem.

Enjoy alone time
You love your friends and being with them, but there's a sigh of relief when you open the door to your empty apartment in the evening.

Likes to meet new people (especially other expats)
You've been around the world and have friends everywhere you've placed a pin on your map.

Comfortable in their own skin
You're happy being you.

'Unstuck'
Here today, gone tomorrow, back to visit.

I'M NEW IN A NEW CITY CHECKLIST

- Clean your apartment (yourself)
- Unpack
- First grocery shop
- Set up utilities
- Connect (phone, internet, etc.)
- Keep an expense report
- Change your postal address
- Integrate with your new community
- Find your local coffee spot
- Create an emergency contact list
- Insure your house contents
- Get a library card
- Sign up for language lessons
- Embrace the new!

PLACES YOU MUST VISIT IN YOUR LIFETIME

Sophisticated yet playful,
romantic and unashamedly full
of clichés: there's no other city in Europe,
let alone the world, quite like the City of Light.
Paris is gothic and yet modern, mysterious and
covertly risqué. Paris is the centre of art, culture and,
of course, fashion. It is home to many lush gardens,
quintessentially Parisian cafés where al fresco
is an institution, and impressive galleries
known the world over. This city is best
seen on foot, so pack your
(chic) comfy shoes!

Musée d'Orsay

Arc de Triomphe

Sainte-Chapelle

Place de la Concorde

Palais Garnier

YOU CAN'T GO TO PARIS AND NOT SEE . . .

Jardin du Luxembourg

Sacré-Cœur

Eiffel Tower

Notre-Dame Cathedral

Louvre

French Language Survival Kit

Bonjour	Hello
Bonsoir	Good evening
Au revoir	Goodbye/See you later
S'il vous plait	Please
Merci	Thank you
Merci beaucoup	Thank you very much
Oui	Yes
Non	No
Tchin-tchin!	Cheers!
Parlez-vous anglais?	Do you speak English?
Madame/Monsieur	Mrs/Mr
Pardon	Pardon me
Excusez-moi!	Sorry!
Je ne comprends pas	I don't understand
Je ne parie pas Français	I don't speak French
Où est le métro?	Where is the subway?
Combien ça coûte	How much does that cost?
Où est la salle de bain?	Where is the bathroom?
Comment vous appelez-vous?	What is your name?
Pouvez-vous m'aider?	Can you help me?

BEST VIEWS

Paris is full of great views, many of them requiring a Euro note and hours in line to enjoy. But one view you won't have to pay for, and that is worth more than any entrance fee, is the Seine River. Whether you visit during the day with cheese and baguettes and a bottle of wine, or you're wandering back to your arrondissement in the late evening under a glittering Eiffel Tower, the Seine River is as undeniably Paris as Paris gets.

Another great (and, better yet, free) view is to be found at the Sacré-Cœur steps and terraces. While here, be sure to visit the neighbourhood of Montmartre — one of the few arrondissements that has managed to retain the feeling and flare of 'old Paris'.

If money isn't an issue, the views worth lining up for include the Arc de Triomphe, the north tower of Notre-Dame and, of course, the Eiffel Tower.

BEST CAFÉS FOR PEOPLE WATCHING IN PARIS

Angelina

Although this is perhaps the most popular and well-known tearoom in Paris, you just can't beat it for a kitsch, but somehow classy, afternoon caffeine hit. If you're after something sweet, opt for the chocolat chaud (hot chocolate) – arguably the best in Paris!

226 Rue de Rivoli, 75001
Métro Tuileries

Café Verlet

Verlet is the place you heard about from a friend of a friend, who was adamant that you must visit next time you are in the neighbourhood. If you're looking for the best coffee in Paris, Café Verlet has been blending since 1880.

256 Rue Saint Honoré, 75001
Métro Palais-Royal Musée du Louvre

Carette

If you're after a sweet treat or just a place to enjoy some of the best al fresco people-watching in Paris, swing by Carette in Place des Vosges.

25 Place des Vosges, 75003
Métro Chemin Vert

Blackburn Coffee

What it lacks in size, it certainly makes up for in style! Blackburn is a more hip alternative to the Parisian café scene and serves great coffee and light bites.

52 Rue du Faubourg Saint-Martin, 75010
Métro Château d'Eau

Café de Flore

While this is one of the most Parisian cafés in Paris, it is also the most well known. It is, however, more than worth a visit to find the Paris you were probably looking for!

172 Boulevard Saint-Germain, 75006
Métro Saint Germain des Près

DAY TRIPS FROM PARIS

Versailles

Versailles is without a shadow of
a doubt the most popular and
worthwhile day trip from Paris.
Opulent, excessive and quite literally
dazzling in the summer sunshine, the
Palace is a reminder of French royalty
as it once was. Be sure not to miss
the gardens, le Petit Trianon (Marie
Antoinette's quarters used for peace
and privacy), the Hall of Mirrors and,
if you have more time, enjoy
a boat ride on the lake in the
summer months.

Chartres

Located just over an hours drive outside
of Paris is Chartres, a charming commune
that is best known for its cathedral – often
referred to as the most striking in all of
France. If taking the train, depart from
Paris Montparnasse and allow up to one
hour and fifteen minutes to arrive.

Château de Fontainebleau

One of the most enviable châteaus in France
is Château de Fontainebleau. Although not as
iconic or well known as Versailles, Fontainebleau
is certainly just as striking. This is a great display
of French architecture both inside and out,
as the Château is filled with history, art,
and classical French beauty at every turn.

Giverny

For art lovers and more specifically
for those who hold an appreciation of
Monet, a visit to Giverny is an absolute
must. Here you can tour the gardens
where the artist dedicated his time and
efforts to his passions: namely, painting,
gardening and photography. Today
the property has been restored and
functions as a museum where visitors
can enjoy the recreated gardens and
an exhibition of some of Monet's most
celebrated works of art.

NEIGHBOURHOODS TO WANDER

The Marais

The Marais is one of the oldest areas in Paris and one of the quaintest neighbourhoods. It's the perfect place for meandering along the many alleyways and backstreets that make this area so charming. The main attraction is Place des Vosges, a public square that is surrounded by great cafes and small art galleries. If you're looking to splurge, Rue Vieille du Temple has a great selection of small boutiques and also some delicious eateries. If you're a fan of crêpes, some of the best in town are to be found at Breizh Café.

St Germain
(Saint-Germain-des-Pres)

Without a shadow of a doubt, St Germain is one of the most charming and quintessentially Parisian neighbourhoods to find yourself in. It is here where you will discover endless cafés and hidden treasures inside the many boutiques and vintage stores. Be sure to give yourself plenty of time; it has long been a favourite of mine and it will soon be one of yours, too!

Montmartre

While it's as pretty as a postcard during the day, the 18th arrondissement isn't somewhere you want to wander around alone at night. Attractions here include Sacré-Cœur, Moulin Rouge and just walking the streets of picturesque Montmartre. One thing you'll notice about the 18th arrondissement is that the food tastes better and costs less. And the views are something to write home about!

The Latin Quarter

The Latin Quarter is a busy part of town with a great eating and drinking scene, ideally situated right next door to St Germain. It should not go unmentioned that the Latin Quarter is also the key neighbourhood for students, and so it is aptly named for the fact that traditionally Latin was the common language among students who came from all over Europe to study in Paris. With student culture comes cheap eats, cheerful streets, and an oversupply of bars to step into for a quick drink, should you fancy one.

IF I HAD TO PICK JUST SIX:
Pâtisseries

Ladurée

As clichéd as it may be, there isn't any reason to deny yourself the guilty pleasure of indulging in French macarons! If pretty pastel plates and even prettier pastries sound like they'll suit your taste, head straight for Ladurée.

21 Rue Bonaparte, 75006 Paris
Métro Saint Germain des Près

Sadaharu AOKI

Sadaharu AOKI is what happens when French pâtisseries blend with the intricacies of Japanese cooking to create a French–Japanese fusion style take on the classics! It extends as far as a wasabi-flavoured macaron – if you dare!

56 Boulevard de Port-Royal, 75005 Paris
Métro Les Gobelins

La Pâtisserie des Rêves

To step things up a notch, make your way to the pâtisserie that rivals them all – where the delights hang in glass homes from the ceilings above. If you get the time, be sure to go out of your way to make it here and try the masterpiece: the Paris-Brest.

111 Rue de Longchamp, 75116 Paris
Métro Rue de la Pompe

Pierre Hermé

This is where you will find arguably the best tasting macarons in all of Paris and perhaps in the entire world. Pierre Hermé is renowned the world over for being inventive and bold, yet still managing to hit the sweet spot with flavour combinations that will leave your mouth watering, in a very literal sense. If there's just one stop to make for a box of take-home macarons, this is it!

72 Rue Bonaparte, 75006 Paris
Métro Saint-Sulpice

Odette

If you find yourself on an eating spree in the Latin quarter and are looking for a sweet pick-me-up afterwards, pop into Odette, a gorgeous sweet shop with a great view towards Notre-Dame. What's on the menu? Skip straight to a choux à la crème (you'll thank me later).

77 Rue Galande, 75005 Paris
Métro Cluny – La Sorbonne

Sébastien Gaudard

This is without a doubt the most imaginative and delicate tearoom you will step inside of in Paris. Every inch is decorated in charming pastels and patterns, so if it's a visual feast you're after, be sure to drop by. Oh, and the food? Incredible.

1 Rue des Pyramides, 75001 Paris | Métro Tuileries

New York is a world in itself.
With skyscrapers towering over the
city that never sleeps and the leafy green
pathways of Central Park, New York will charm
you in more ways than one. From the coffee culture
of Williamsburg through to the blow-outs of
the Upper East, each of New York's little
pockets will fulfil its stereotype yet
simultaneously shock you. That's
the beauty of this city!

The High Line

Times Square

Museum of Modern Art

Grand Central Terminal

Top of
the Rock

TOP SPOTS

Central
Park

Statue of Liberty

The Metropolitan
Museum of Art

Brooklyn Bridge

Empire State
Building

95

BEST FOOD TRUCKS IN NYC

Sweetery NYC

While most food trucks go for the guilty pleasures of warm comfort foods with all the trimmings, the Sweetery NYC food truck skips straight to dessert. One waft as you walk down the street will likely lure you in to see all the delicious make-your-own croissants and pastries, and there are even baked savoury goods!

433 W 34th St, New York
@SweeteryNYC

Gorilla Cheese NYC

Two words: grilled cheese. Gorilla Cheese is precisely where you'll find the best kind of comfort food – grilled cheese sandwiches and for an incredibly cheap price. Locations change all the time so be sure to check their social media to keep up on all the action.

@gcnyc1

Wafels & Dinges

Wafels & Dinges is a food truck so popular that they've opened a flagship location in the city! Be sure to come hungry as the portion sizes are beyond belief, and don't be surprised if both a savoury and sweet waffle menu item take your fancy. If you can't find one of the food trucks, head straight for W 35th Street to visit the shop.

433 W 34th St, New York
@waffletruck

Korilla BBQ

One of the most popular food trucks in New York City, Korilla BBQ started as a single food truck selling authentic Korean BBQ cuisine and now there are a string of food trucks all over the city. Vegetarians are also catered for with, yep, you guessed it . . . tofu!

23 3rd Ave, New York
@korillaBBQ

NEIGHBOURHOODS TO WANDER

There is much more to NYC than the area around Times Square. And I absolutely forbid you to class a stroll across Brooklyn Bridge as a visit to Brooklyn! Here are some of my personal favourite neighbourhoods to wander around and get lost in.

Flatiron District/Union Square

This neighbourhood is most commonly marked by the not-to-be-missed Flatiron Building. Around the area (Union Square is located at 5th Avenue, from 14th to 17th Street), there are oodles of great shops, restaurants, quick eats and the renowned Union Square Greenmarket, where you will find a great selection of fresh food.

East Village

While this area was once an edgy neighbourhood popular with immigrants, it has gentrified over the years and is now a more watered-down version of itself. However, it is still extremely culturally diverse. Here you will find 'Little India', home to some excellent (and also cheap) restaurants featuring Eastern cooking. East Village is a great neighbourhood to explore and graze your way around.

DUMBO

Another literal name, DUMBO was named for its location 'Down Under the Manhattan Bridge Overpass'. This neighbourhood in Brooklyn offers fantastic views of the Manhattan skyline. Better yet, DUMBO is just a short walk from the Brooklyn Bridge!

Meatpacking District

Also known as Gansevoort Market, the Meatpacking District was once, as the name suggests, an industrial area full of warehouses where wholesale meat companies operated. Nowadays it is a popular residential area with expensive boutiques and an incredibly popular nightclub scene. It is also here that you will find the High Line park – one of the most popular parks in the city, opened in the summer of 2009.

SoHo & Tribeca

SoHo was given its name as it is 'South of Houston Street', while Tribeca is 'the Triangle Below Canal Street'! These areas are popular for shopping and galleries and have fantastic loft apartments (a girl can dream, right!?), and a booming café scene with many great healthy eateries.

NoHo/Nolita

NoHo is 'North of Houston Street'. This area has become popular over the years as an alternative to SoHo, after boutique designers were pushed out by rising rent prices and just happened to move right next door! There are some fabulous local stores on offer in this area, which feels a world away from the branded streets of SoHo.

Williamsburg

Across the Williamsburg Bridge from Manhattan is one of the most popular residential areas of Brooklyn: Williamsburg. The area is young and full of hipsters who have sought out the best of both worlds by being outside of the hustle and bustle of Manhattan, while still having everything they need to keep themselves entertained in this thriving neighbourhood.

Chinatown & Little Italy

This is where you will find all the fantastic food and drink in the city that won't leave you with empty pockets. Both Chinatown and Little Italy really come to life in the evenings, so be sure to visit after dark. This is a great place to meander with a group of friends, or just to position yourself at one of the many al fresco dining offerings and enjoy the outdoor ambience.

Greenwich Village/West Village

Greenwich Village, also known as West Village, is one of the most popular residential areas to live in as it is filled with beautiful townhouses, lush leafy streets, and a quaint neighbourhood vibe. Washington Square Park is one of my favourite spots to stop for a lazy afternoon picnic or book read in the sun, and it is also highly popular among New York University students, as the university campuses are nearby. Here you will also be able to find an endless array of food options including famous New York-style pizza, cupcakes, hotdogs, falafel sandwiches and much more!

As one of the most
popular cities for travellers
to visit, London has a lot on offer.
While there's more to London than its
famous sights and attractions, you still shouldn't
come to London without seeing them, if only once
in your life. Be sure to swing by Buckingham Palace
for the changing of the guard, enjoy afternoon tea
at a fancy hotel, learn the history of London
at the Tower of London and Tower Bridge,
and embrace modernity atop The
Shard building for the best
views over London.

Tower of London

Buckingham Palace

Tower Bridge

British Museum

London Eye

TOP SPOTS

Big Ben

Palace of Westminster

Westminster Abbey

Portobello Road Market

St Paul's Cathedral

10 INCREDIBLE HOTELS IN LONDON

London is one of the world's most expensive cities but for the quintessential British experience, you've gotta go all out. If I had a winning lottery ticket, here's where I'd check myself into (or, at the very least, book myself in for a fancy afternoon tea!):

The Stafford London

Traditional and stylish, The Stafford welcomes a pretty impressive guest list and I'm not just talking about the guests who stay there: royals themselves have been spotted sneaking in for lunch meetings. The rooms are also as British as they come, so much so that you would be forgiven for thinking you're in the English countryside, not one of the busiest cities in the world.

thestaffordlondon.com

The Dorchester

Overlooking Hyde Park is the highly celebrated Dorchester Hotel, renowned for its 1930s furnishings that, despite modernisation, would lead you to believe you've transported back in time. Even if you aren't staying at the hotel, be sure to stroll by and strike up a conversation with the lovely English chaps on the door – you can't miss 'em!

dorchestercollection.com/en/london

The Lanesborough

This striking hotel overlooks Hyde Park and has a certain unique charm that is hard to resist. Classic but with a refreshing appeal, The Lanesborough will impress even the most discerning traveller.

lanesborough.com

Claridge's

Location is everything in London and the position of Claridge's is as good as it gets. Located in Mayfair (yup, the expensive part of the monopoly board) and just a short stroll to the Oxford Street shops, Claridge's is an art deco icon.

claridges.co.uk

Dukes Hotel

Home to the bar that inspired Ian Fleming's 'shaken not stirred' sentiment in the James Bond stories, Dukes is an intimate affair with wingback chairs and a swanky champagne bar. Pop in for a martini!

dukeshotel.com

The Ritz London

The Ritz not only hosts a daily but a multiple-sittings-per-day afternoon tea to rival that on offer at Buckingham Palace itself. Set on Piccadilly, this uber-luxe hotel is often regarded as one of the finest in London.

theritzlondon.com

The Milestone Hotel

While many of the hotels listed are positioned in what is some of the most expensive real estate in town, the local Londoners will tell you that the really swanky area is over in Kensington, Knightsbridge and Chelsea. It is here where you will find The Milestone, a timeless and effortlessly classic hotel with more character than you could possibly imagine.

milestonehotel.com

The Savoy

Famously situated on the Strand, this is one hotel that commands the attention of every passer-by. The location of the hotel also makes it the perfect base for exploring the city's hot spots. It's not more than a ten-minute walk from Trafalgar Square and a little further onwards you'll find the London Eye and many other attractions.

fairmont.com/savoy-london

41

Located on Buckingham Palace Road, it is little wonder 41 is one of the most sought-after hotels in London. Stepping inside the black-and-white tiled foyer is just the beginning as the astute doorman accompanies you to the lift to uncover what's behind those rich mahogany doors.

41hotel.com

The Goring

The Goring is so famous that it has managed to successfully drop 'hotel' from its name, a testament to its reputation as one of London's finest family-run hotels. The lush hedge trimmings that line that entrance are worth seeing in themselves!

thegoring.com

NEIGHBOURHOODS TO WANDER

London is often thought to be red phone boxes, black cabs, afternoon tea and Buckingham Palace. Sure, it is all of these things . . . but also so much more! Branch out to some of my favourite neighbourhoods to see what lies beyond the tourist attractions. (Trust me, you'll soon see why you can never spend enough time in this city!)

Soho

Located in central London, Soho is quirky and still a little bit seedy, though one of the most happening evening neighbourhoods in London. Here you will find a hub of restaurants, pubs, bars, private clubs and even plenty of pop-up food stalls throughout the warmer months. If you're looking for a place to dance well into the night, Soho is a great choice for a fun night out.

Chelsea

Chelsea is one of the most affluent neighbourhoods in the city. It is home to the 'posh kids', those with the perfect British accents, Victorian homes, fancy cars . . . you get my drift. It is, however, a gorgeous place to wander around and has some fantastic little cafes to sit back in and people-watch. Favourite choices include The Good Life Eatery, Tom's Kitchen and No. 11 Pimlico Road.

Brooke

Shoreditch

Located in East London, Shoreditch is a grungier area where you can spend your day sifting through vintage thrift stores, sipping on the best coffee in town, and rubbing shoulders with the hippest of hipsters, especially on weekends when this neighbourhood is buzzing with life!

Notting Hill

Just as the film portrays it, Notting Hill is a quaint and delightful neighbourhood that is home to artists, markets and, of course, the famous Portobello Road. While it is now a very upmarket part of the city to reside in, it has still managed to retain much of its charm, especially on Saturdays when tourists and locals alike flock to the Portobello Road Market.

BEST DAY TRIPS

Bath

Bath is set in the rolling English countryside and is famous for its eighteenth-century Georgian architecture and thermal hot springs. Be sure to visit the Roman Baths, Royal Crescent, the Circus, and Bath Abbey. There are plenty of great attractions to keep you busy for a day, however, if you wish to combine a day trip to Bath with Windsor Castle and Stonehenge, that is also entirely possible!

Oxford

Just one and a half hours outside of London is the gorgeous university town of Oxford. This is a very popular day trip as it has been home to many of the world's most renowned scholars and gives a great insight into the history of university studies. For fans of Lewis Caroll and the *Harry Potter* films, there is plenty to see and do here. Connections are seamless with buses and trains departing frequently in both directions.

The Cotswolds

If you're looking for quaint, cutesy and charming Britain, head straight for the Cotswolds region. These little villages are a delight to see, but you will need a car to get around. This is a great day trip if you want to explore and unwind in the English countryside.

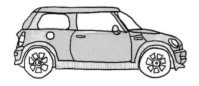

BEST BRUNCH

Granger & Co.

Arguably the best brunch in London can be found at Granger & Co. This brunch haunt has refined the art of hot breakfasts – from eggs to pancakes and everything in between, each meal is a work of art, plated and placed right before your very eyes.

The Good Life Eatery

This café is renowned as a local favourite. With an impressive egg menu and a selection of vegan options available, they have something for everyone. The Good Life Eatery embrace superfoods like they were sent to earth on a mission to do so – and, boy, do they do a good job!

Dishoom

Dishoom is another fantastic brunch spot that, due to its success, has now expanded to multiple locations across London. With a strong Indian influence accompanied by inspiration from all over the world, eating at Dishoom can feel as if you're escaping London through whatever is on your plate.

M1lk

If you're looking for a declicious brunch south of the river, make a trip to M1lk. The sweet corn fritters are a hit and, of course, true to their name, they specialise in drinks, especially great coffee.

Gail's Kitchen

Now with numerous locations throughout London, Gail's was one of the pioneers in bringing the art of brunching to London. Known for their bread, Gail's is a bakery as well as the perfect common workspace and another great brunch option.

Venice is precisely as you imagined. The films, photos and postcards are entirely reflective of what you will find here: canals, singing gondoliers, palaces, churches, magnificent architecture in a variety of styles, and more history than you'll be able to absorb. It would be indulgent to complain about the hoards of tourists, scorching summer sun and long queues — because that is what you'd get in any major city in Europe. Besides, it's entirely worth it for the melting ice-cream!

Bridge of Sighs

Teatro La Fenice

Doge's Palace

Rialto Bridge

Gallerie dell'Accademia

Murano

TOP SPOTS

Grand Canal

Saint Mark's Basilica

Dorsoduro

Piazza San Marco

Italian Language Survival Kit

Ciao	Hello
Buona sera	Good evening
Arrivederci	Goodbye
Per favour	Please
Grazie	Thank you
Grazile mille	Thank you very much
Si	Yes
No	No
Saluti!	Cheers!
Lei parla inglese?	Do you speak English?
Signora/Signor	Mrs/Mr
Scusami	Pardon me
Scusa!	Sorry!
Non capisco	I don't understand
Lo non parlo Italiano	I don't speak Italian
Dove è la metropolitana?	Where is the subway?
Quanto costa?	How much does that cost?
Dove è il bagno?	Where is the bathroom?
Come ti chiami?	What is your name?
Mi potete aiutare?	Can you help me?

VENICE HIGHLIGHTS

Oct. 2006
Tourist Office
ENTUM LIBE...
VALID 30 DAYS STAY...
669 DATE OF ARR...
9 - 11 . 2016

Carnival of Venice

Most famous for its traditional Venetian masks, the Carnival of Venice is an annual event that brings the city to life as colourful costumes, and personalities take to the streets. If you happen to be in the city during this time, then be prepared for a spectacle, with masses of party-goers bursting through the city to pose, dance and be merry. Worried about that all-important 'But what will I wear?'question? Fear not! You can rent costumes for the festival and even attend fancy masked balls in the evenings.

Souvenirs

Venice is one city in Europe where it's permissible to stock your suitcase full of souvenirs to take home. However, I'm not talking about snow globes and key chains. Venice is full of traditional handicrafts that will leave a lasting impression, like Venetian masks and Murano glass, lace and linens. Be sure to seek out reputable sellers, as quality differs substantially.

An Art Walk

From Titian to Tintoretto, Tiepolo and everyone in between, there are fantastic museums housing great historic and contemporary artists in Venice. But art is everywhere – on the pavement, in the façades and, of course, the impressive architecture. So be sure to explore Venice as much as possible on foot (granted, it is almost your only option in many places). Museums not to be missed include the Gallerie dell'Accademia, Ca' Rezzonico, Galleria Giorgio Franchetti alla Ca d'Oro, Peggy Guggenheim Collection, and the Punta della Dogana.

WHERE TO TAKE THE BEST PHOTOS OF VENICE

People often ask me if the places I've been are as pretty as the postcards, and for Venice I always say yes. Sure, it is full of tourists and bird poop, and often reaches sweltering heats that would make it tempting to skinny-dip in the Grand Canal. But Venice is playful, colourful, impossibly romantic and a maze of discovery. Here's where to go to capture that side of the city:

St Mark's Campanile, Piazza San Marco

A city as sprawling as Venice needs to be viewed from above and there is no better place to get on top of Venice than the peak of the bell tower. At 160 metres high, you will be able to view the thousands of terracotta rooftops in the distance, all glistening in the morning light. From here you can get a full 360-degree view over the city, so be sure to stay as long as you need to capture all that lies beneath you.

Palazzo Ducale, San Marco

If you came to Venice to photograph the Venetian Gothic architecture that draws millions of visitors each year, then you simply must go to Palazzo Ducale (Doge's Palace). Early morning is the best time to capture this masterpiece.

Getting lost

The only way to get a photo of Venice that hasn't been taken a million times before is to lose yourself in the maze that is Venice. Simply by wandering away from the busy tourist streets you will find yourself exposed to the real Venice, where residents live, hang out their washing and take their small dogs for a walk. It is here where you will discover a deeper side beyond the hot spots, top attractions and basically everything you can read about in a guidebook. So go on, get lost!

It's all in the details

One of the most difficult aspects of capturing Venice is the sunlight. Expect long, hot and often sticky days, which are only made worse by the never-ending stream of tourists (especially in the summer; don't expect any elbow room!). During the middle of the day when the light is glaring and the heat is starting to take its toll, head indoors and capture the details. Look out for intricacies such as the designs of the Venetian masks, lace, or the art of glass-making.

From the canals on a gondola

There is one experience that you just cannot come to Venice and do without: riding in a gondola. It really is as cheesy, cringe-worthy and smirk-inducing as the movies have led you to believe . . . which just gives you more reason to do it! From a gondola you can capture the true essence of Venice: bursting with colour, life, singing gondoliers and decaying buildings. All of it – the good and the bad – make up Venice as it is today. Embrace it!

St Petersburg is a city
that will charm the pants off
any critic and leave you in awe of the
longstanding history of Eastern Europe.
While Western Europe often takes all the glory,
there is so much on offer in St Petersburg. The Hermitage
museum rivals the collection of the Louvre, the canals
of St Petersburg are like those of Venice on a much
grander scale, and the impressive summer
residence of Peter the Great, Peterhof,
showcases the legacy the Tsars have
left on the state of Russia.

ST PETERSBURG

NEVA RIVER

VODKA

The State
Hermitage
Museum

Peterhof Palace

Saint Isaac's Cathedral

Mariinsky
Theatre

TOP SPOTS

Church
of Our Savior
on the
Spilled Blood

Peter and Paul Fortress

Admiralty building

Russian Museum

Kazan Cathedral

Summer Garden

Catherine Palace

Russian Language Survival Kit

Zdravstvuyte	Hello
Dobryy vecher	Good evening
Proshchay	Goodbye
Pozhaluysta	Please
Spasibo	Thank you
Bol'shoye spasibo	Thank you very much
Da	Yes
Net	No
Ura!	Cheers!
Ty govorish' po-angliyski?	Do you speak English?
Mister/G-zha	Mr/Mrs
Prostite	Pardon me
Prosti!	Sorry!
Ya ne ponimayu	I don't understand
Ya ne govoryu Russkiy	I don't speak Russian
Gde nakhoditsya stantsiya metro?	Where is the metro station?
Skol'ko eto stoit?	How much does that cost?
Gde zdes' vannaya komnata?	Where is the bathroom?
Kak vas zovut?	What is your name?
Mozhesh' mne pomoch?	Can you help me?

THINGS TO DO/SEE

Visiting the State Hermitage Museum

St Petersburg is full of exciting attractions both indoors and out, but there's no denying that the most all-encompassing of these is the famed State Hermitage Museum, arguably the most impressive museum in the world. Catherine the Great, the longest reigning Empress of Russia, founded the Hermitage. Nowadays the museum houses an impressive collection, with over three million items on display. But this isn't just another museum to wander around and show half-hearted interest in – the entire building itself is much like an exhibition. The rooms are dazzling, with crystal chandeliers, gold trimmings, marble, timber and an array of the best furnishings from around the world.

TIPS FOR YOUR VISIT:

- Do allow yourself at least half a day here as there is much to see. Better yet, see the collections over a couple of days rather than trying to squeeze everything in at once.

- The queue dies down around lunchtime so this is often the best time to enter.

- When queuing, check that you are in the correct line, as one line is for groups and another is for individuals.

- You can purchase tickets online. However, tickets are cheaper at the entrance gate.

- No matter which way you go about it, you are bound to get lost at some point within your visit.

White Nights

Every year during midsummer, roughly between between June 11 and July 2, the White Nights (Beliye Nochi) arrive in St Petersburg, when the summer sun lasts long into the evenings creating an all-night glow. Put simply, the whole twenty-four hours of the day over these brief weeks are lit by sunlight, leading to the name 'White Nights'. This is a great time to visit St Petersburg to see it truly come to life, as there are often people on the streets at all hours of the day and night enjoying this phenomenon.

Mariinsky Theatre

The acclaimed Mariinsky Theatre is the historic home of theatrical opera and ballet in St Petersburg. The theatre has held this position since the late nineteenth century and has long welcomed royalty and affluent Russians to its private boxes. The interior itself is incredibly impressive and is worth a visit for its own sake, but don't forget that the operas and ballets on offer here are some of the best in the world.

If there's one thing the Russians don't get enough credit for, it's their cuisine. While some of it may be a little hard to stomach (I mean, there are only so many dumplings you can squeeze in), much of it is delicious and, at the very least, worth a try.

Russian pancakes (blini)

Better known as 'blini' to those in the West, Russian pancakes are so important to the culture that there's a Russian Pancake Week (Maslenitsa) every year before Lent begins. Now that's my kinda week!

Russian dumplings (pelmeni)

In my humble opinion it is hard to visit any country that specialises in dumplings and not make it a top priority to conduct a full taste test. Russian dumplings are typically filled with herbed meat, not a great option for the vegetarians of the world, though if you dig deep enough you'll be able to find some vegetarian options in St Petersburg.

Sbiten

If you fancy a hot drink then you just might like to try the Russian take on a winter warm-me-up: sbiten. The drink is a mix of honey, spices and jam. It is sweet with a heavy dose of spice, making it the perfect daily companion if you're visiting St Petersburg during the colder months.

Stroganoff

I've spent half of my life as a vegetarian, but there are few dishes I remember quite as well as stroganoff, a Russian classic that has been served in my family for years. Essentially this dish consists of sautéed beef and a thick, creamy sauce. Given that it is entirely non-vegetarian, I didn't try my luck on the real deal in St Petersburg, but for the meat-eaters out there this dish is about as bona fide as it gets!

Honeycake (medovik)

For my own safety, I didn't try medovik when I was in Russia for fear of a self-induced sugar coma that I would possibly never come out of. Due to my inability to know when enough is enough, I do my best to avoid sweet treats wherever possible, but the honeycake is on my radar for my next visit. This treat features crispy baked layers of cake with sour cream frosting in between . . . definitely sounds worth a try!

Vodka

Of course it needs no introduction, but can we all just pause for a moment and appreciate the novelty of drinking vodka in Russia? Chances are you won't be able to keep up with the Russians, so I would (for safety and legal reasons) strongly advise against doing so, but if you do get the chance to drop into a bar in St Petersburg, be sure to remember that there is only one drink of choice on offer.

3.

SEE IT
WITH YOUR
OWN EYES

WONDERS
OF THE
WORLD

Grand Bazaar, Istanbul

As one of the oldest markets in the world, Istanbul's Grand Bazaar is truly as close as one might come to stepping back in time. The colourful spice market, the charming lampshades in every colour of the rainbow and the trinkets to sift through are just the start of this magic carpet ride through enchanting Istanbul!

Machu Picchu, Peru

As you walk through the remains of the Inca civilisation at Machu Picchu, high up in the clouds, you cannot help but be transported back thousands of years. The hardcore travellers will choose to take the multi-day trek leading to Machu Picchu, but don't be ashamed to opt for the train ride to the top for a day visit; you'll be equally impressed.

Angkor Wat, Siem Reap

Wandering through the temples of Angkor Wat is about as close as I will ever come to being Lara Croft, even if I was meandering through the temples in a pair of sneakers and a summer playsuit. Yes, it is as pretty as the pictures, and yes, you'll see many monkeys! Hooray for monkeys!

Times Square, New York City

While it is a far cry from the most cultural or charming pockets of New York City, it is certainly a must-visit at least once in your life. The first time you see Times Square should be at night, with the flashing lights illuminating the skies above, allowing you to let your eyes dart around 360 degrees. This is one place where it's okay to play up the kitsch. So go on, buy a burger or a hotdog and eat on the street as you let the world pass you by. There's no judgement here.

Moai statues, Easter Island

Lying remotely in the Pacific Ocean is the volcanic Easter Island, home to the iconic moai statues that have mystified historians and archaeologists for centuries. This is easily one of the world's most recognisable but least-visited sites, thanks to its remote location, over 3500 kilometres from the Chilean mainland.

Christ the Redeemer, Rio de Janeiro

Before arriving in Rio de Janeiro, you could be forgiven for thinking it is merely the city with the Christ the Redeemer statue overlooking it – this is all that came to mind for me before I arrived. I've now learned my lesson! There's so much to Rio beyond this iconic statue, but you can't come to Rio without seeing it (and if you didn't get a photo – did you even go?).

Colosseum, Rome

I never understood the function of the Colosseum until I watched the film *Gladiator*. While I'm not sure how accurate this depiction is (Hollywood has a way of juicing things up), I quite fancied the film and it single-handedly led me to want to visit the site. Russell Crowe and his counterparts depict the horrific events that took place here, including gladiators fighting one another, wild animal fights, and a mixture of the two. Crazy how far we've come in history, ain't it?

Sydney Opera House, Sydney

In many ways the Sydney Opera House is the icon of Australia. This is the location made famous when New Year's Eve festivities are broadcast all over the world, as Australia is one of the first countries to bring in the New Year. I most enjoy the view that sits directly behind it, the Sydney Harbour itself. This is one of the few big cities in the world that doesn't feel chaotic or cramped at all, especially in the harbour part of town.

Fushimi Inari-taisha shrine, Kyoto

Fushimi Inari-taisha is an incredible, seemingly endless, maze of bright red torii gates that act as a tunnel leading toward the sacred Mount Inari. Kyoto is full of colourful sights and insights that will transport you back thousands of years to ancient Japan, but none are more striking than these beautiful gates!

St Peter's Basilica, Vatican City

If there's just one thing I remember most clearly from my visit to the Vatican, it's the guard uniforms that resemble jokers' outfits (oh so stylish). But, seriously, the Vatican is a unique place to visit, particularly St Peter's Basilica in all of its grandeur. The main façade is enough to knock you off your feet if you're new to Italy, however if you're already well versed in Renaissance architecture, then just give yourself a moment to step inside and, I promise you, you'll have a hard time forgetting those interiors any time soon.

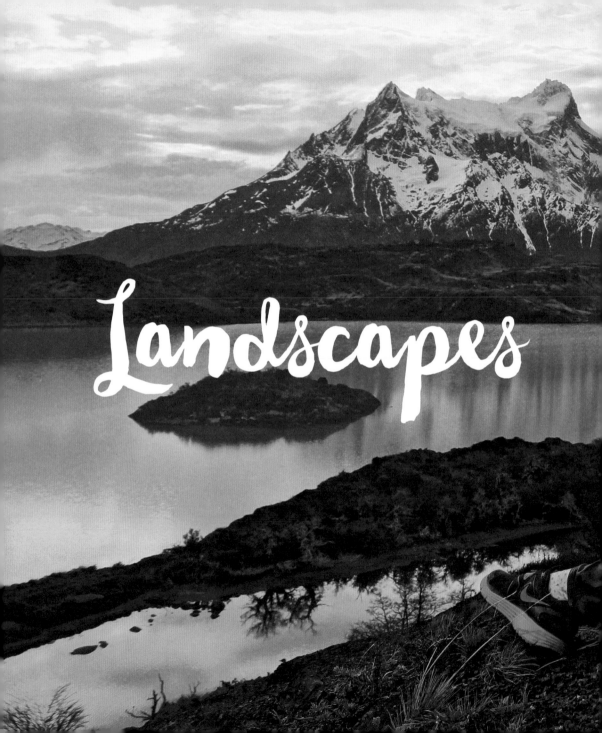

Landscapes

Torres del Paine, Chile

Torres del Paine National Park is perhaps the single-most stunning landscape to be found in the world (according to me, at least). Located in southern Chile's Patagonia region, the area is full to the brim with blue icebergs, glaciers and rare wildlife, such as pumas. While in Patagonia be sure to squeeze in as many activities as possible, especially trekking and horse riding, two of my favourite travel memories from South America!

Zhangye Danxia Landform, China

China is on most travellers' bucket lists for a few notable places (I'm thinking about a wall that is great, a city that is forbidden . . .) but what many don't know is that China is home to some incredible landscapes, including the Zhangye Danxia Landform. You don't have to be into geology to appreciate it, though. You'll merely need to be fond of bright, colourful, pretty things!

Plitvice Lakes National Park, Croatia

The Plitvice Lakes National Park has been on my 'go to' list for a while and I'm eager to discover it before the crowds start arriving in bus loads (which, according to my sources, makes me already too late). The park is now one of the main tourist attractions in Croatia, alongside the renowned seaside city of Dubrovnik – another must, especially for *Game of Thrones* fans!

Arashiyama Bamboo Groves, Japan

Hidden like a tranquil oasis in a quiet neighborhood on the outskirts of Kyoto, Arashiyama's Bamboo Groves are like stepping into another world: one where nature reigns supreme and the sky is the limit! Arrive early before the crowds to really enjoy the serenity, when the morning sun peeking through the bamboo will bring this magical place to life.

Horseshoe Bend, Arizona, USA

The Colorado River wends its way through a number of southwestern states in the USA and northern Mexico, but nowhere is it more impressive (at least in my eyes) than at Horseshoe Bend in northern Arizona, just a short drive from the small town of Page. There the river bends in the shape of a horseshoe earning the site its iconic reputation. Be sure to visit at golden hour, just an hour before sunset, for an extra dose of magic when the red rocks light up with the setting sun in the background.

Plateau de Valensole, France

If you're ever stuck in a rut and looking for an out, type the phrase 'Alpes-de-haute-Provence lavender fields' into an internet search engine and prepare for instant envy. These lush fields are best viewed in full bloom in the summer sunshine, with July being the most popular month to visit.

Yosemite, California, USA

There are so many incredible national parks in the United States but I'll never forget my winter wonderland visit to California's Yosemite National Park. Covered in a thick layer of snow, the mountains appeared ethereal in the distance and the earth beneath was a winter playground! With frozen waterfalls and the occasional snow flake, you really can't stay indoors despite the cold temperatures!

Cappadocia, Turkey

If the word 'Cappadocia' immediately makes you think of oodles of hot air balloons in a colourful pastel sky, then you'll know just how much eye candy is coming into my imagination while I write these words. Cappadocia is an incredible landscape best seen from the sky, in a sea of hot air balloons no less!

Salar de Uyuni, Bolivia

I went to Bolivia for one reason and one reason alone – to see the salt flats, more formally known as Salar de Uyuni. I was staying in La Paz, the capital of Bolivia, and, to my extreme disappointment following an extremely unfortunate series of events, did not make it down to Uyuni, despite having a bus ticket in hand, accommodation and a tour of the salt flats booked. So what did I learn from this? Expect the unexpected, especially in South America!

Aurora Borealis, Northern Hemisphere

The *Aurora Borealis* is nature's version of an impressive light show that will leave you in awe and at a loss for words. When travelling through Finnish Lapland a couple of years ago I saw the lights on one of my last evenings in the area, spending the hour that followed completely spellbound by this natural phenomenon. The lights are most commonly seen in Alaska, Canada, Greenland, Iceland, Norway, Sweden and Finland . . . so start planning!

TRAVEL
TIPS

Determine your budget so that you know what you can and can't afford when planning your trip.

Start saving! You have to start somewhere.

Research your flights on flight comparison search engines to find the cheapest fare.

If you can't afford travel insurance, you can't afford to travel.

Crosscheck accommodation booking sites for the cheapest rates.

Research activities and day trips in advance but hold off on booking in case you change your mind or find a better alternative once you arrive.

NOTES ON PLANNING

See your doctor to check if you need any immunisations and act accordingly.

Advise your banks you will be travelling in order to avoid your accounts being frozen.

Plan a rough itinerary so you know you can fit everything in but don't be afraid to stray from it.

If you haven't already, sign up to Pinterest. Start pinning travel shots and follow travel accounts that will give you inspiration.

Give a copy of your itinerary to your family as a safety precaution.

MONEY MATTERS

Research ways to save money on things such as flights, accommodation, activities, and more. Sign up for alerts for flight sales, hotel sales, package sales, etc.

Staying in places longer will save money thanks to hotel deals or week-long apartment rentals.

Don't be afraid to grab food on the go or opt for a supermarket meal for dinner (cheese and crackers are my fave go-to). No judgement here!

Don't skimp on everything. Be sure to splurge when it is something you know you will never get the chance to do again, like a music concert, a local attraction or an activity you have always wanted to try.

Your main travel budget should consist of flights, travel insurance, accommodation and a daily allowance.

The more money you have set aside, the better!

ADMITTED
NEW
APR 06 2009
Class
Until

PLANNING AN EXTRAORDINARY ADVENTURE

(A Checklist)

Going on an adventure? You'll need a few things.

DOCUMENTS

- Passport
- Photocopy and scan of first page of passport
- Visa
- Driver's licence or secondary form of ID
- Currency or bank card (or both)
- Confirmations – flights, hotels, etc.
- Travel insurance policy number

CLOTHING/ FOOTWEAR

- Active wear – wicking t-shirt, pants, underwear
- T-shirt (2)
- Cap or hat
- Swimsuit
- Rain jacket
- Insulating jacket
- Gloves or mittens
- Casual clothes
- Hiking boots
- Sneakers
- Socks (2)
- Underwear (2)

RANDOM

- Water bottle
- Headlamp or flashlight
- Binoculars
- Battery charger(s) and tech charger(s)
- Multi-tool
- Camera
- Memory card
- Extra batteries
- Book(s)
- Language phrasebook/App
- Headphones
- Journal

LUGGAGE

- Travel pack or suitcase
- Duffel bag – for carry on or short adventures
- Day pack
- Camera bag(s)
- Computer bag
- Resealable plastic bags
- Luggage lock
- Luggage tag

PERSONAL

- Sunglasses
- Sunscreen
- Lip balm
- Insect repellent
- Hand sanitizer
- Skin lotion
- Medications
- Toiletry kit
- Toothbrush
- Toothpaste
- Cosmetics
- Hair brush
- Earplugs
- Eye mask

Ensure you pack comfortable, worn-in shoes.

Place a ribbon or baggage tag on your bag to avoid grabbing the wrong one at the conveyer belt.

Pack a change of clothes, toothbrush, toothpaste and deodorant in your carry-on luggage in case of lost luggage.

Make a checklist.

Don't forget your prescription medicine and ensure it is clearly labelled.

Pack a small first-aid kit with headache tablets.

NOTES ON PACKING

Don't forget an adaptor – a universal one if you're travelling to a number of countries!

Weigh your bag before you leave and be sure to leave at least 5 kilograms spare for purchases abroad!

Once you have packed your bags, take everything back out and remove at least five items. Leave at home anything you might not need, will only wear once or could buy while you're there.

THE SECRET TO LEARNING A NEW LANGUAGE

If you've ever tried to learn a new language, you'll know firsthand that it doesn't happen overnight. But it is still possible to master a new language as you get older, especially if you know the secret to doing so.

It takes a little bit of practice each and every day. **Consistency** – the key to learning a new language!

Make it a daily habit

Consistency is a challenge in a world where nearly everyone and everything is constantly calling for your attention, but it truly is the only way to teach yourself a new language. By making it a habit to spend 30–60 minutes each day learning more of your new language, you will slowly but surely teach yourself new words without losing all the knowledge you've already gained. Practice makes perfect!

Use technology

It is now easier than ever to learn a new language with so many apps and online tools available to us, all just one click away. Choose the one that works best for you and stick with it!

Practise everywhere, all the time

The most common reason people cannot retain the language they are trying to learn is because they aren't practising in real-life situations. That's why they say the best way to learn a language is in a country where it is spoken. Don't be discouraged! You are capable of learning a new language regardless of where you are, you just have to be willing to practise out loud everywhere, all the time.

Don't be afraid to make mistakes

When conversing with someone in the foreign language you are trying to learn, never be afraid of making mistakes – mistakes are how you learn! Also, don't get too caught up in how you sound in comparison to other native speakers as the accent will come with time.

Learn in more ways than one

Finally, the best way to master a new language is to do all of the above and learn in more ways than one. Read it, speak it, listen to it, watch it on television and do whatever you can to immerse yourself in the language you are trying to learn. Persistence pays off!

GUIDE TO AIRPORT STYLE

When I was a little girl my grandmother told me that going on a plane meant wearing your Sunday best. 'You never know who you might meet on an aeroplane!' she would tell me. Although air travel is much more common nowadays, I always try to look my best whenever I board a plane, striking a personal balance between comfort and chic.

Loose fit

When trying to catch some zzz's on a fourteen-hour flight, the last thing you want to feel is restricted. Whatever you wear, make sure the top and pants are loose fitting so that you can manoeuvre yourself into that crazy sleeping position that just somehow works.

Boots vs. sneakers

It goes without saying that planes aren't the most hygienic of places, especially when making your way to a lavatory that might not have been cleaned throughout the entire flight. To avoid any unwanted germs, be sure to wear closed-toe shoes on board. I personally love to wear boots as they look stylish with a pair of jeans or pants, but you will have to remove them when passing through security checks so if you're not one to waste time, perhaps consider sneakers!

Jeans vs. trousers

For the purpose of keeping warm on board, I will never board a flight in anything other than trousers. Jeans are a good choice if you have a pair that fit well and don't restrict you when you're sitting down. However, if you haven't yet found a comfy pair of jeans then any trousers will do the trick!

Black is best

My first trick for staying stylish in transit is to always keep it neutral with dark tones. Eating on a plane or in airports immediately renders pale colours out of the question. Stick to black or dark colours in your outfit choice.

The secret is in how you feel on the inside

Style is just one part of looking and feeling good in an airport. The other huge consideration is how you feel on the inside. Be sure to drink plenty of water on the day of flying – before you depart, on board, and after your flight. Eat light meals and prepare your own snacks beforehand in case you don't like the food on board.

Layers, layers, layers

If there's one thing I know to be true about air travel, it's that airlines love to either crank up the air-conditioning, or not crank it at all! The safest bet is to wear a number of layers, such as a singlet top, loose fitting top, jacket and scarf, to ensure you stay warm, but can cool down as needed.

Sunglasses in your handbag

Sometimes it just isn't possible to combat jetlag. Personally I have found the best cure to be staying awake in your new time zone when you arrive. Often that means tired, weary and baggy eyes...so be sure to pack a pair of sunglasses to hide behind!

Great Plane Reads

The Great Railway Bazaar by Paul Theroux, 1975

Gulliver's Travels by Jonathan Swift, 1726

Into the Wild by Jon Krakauer, 1996

Along the Ganges by Ilija Trojanow, 2003

Paris Letters by Janice MacLeod, 2014

The Innocents Abroad by Mark Twain, 1869

A Walk in the Woods by Bill Bryson, 1998

A Year in the Merde by Stephen Clarke, 1985

A Thousand Days in Tuscany by Marlena de Blasi, 2004

The Good Girl's Guide to Getting Lost by Rachel Friedman, 2011

POUTINE

CANADA

Pizza

ITALY

ALFAJORES

SPAIN

Macarons

FRANCE

Frites

BELGIUM

Pho

VIETNAM

FOOD TO TRAVEL THE WORLD FOR

Falafel

EGYPT

CRÊPES

FRANCE

MINT TEA

MOROCCO

Green Curry

THAILAND

Gelati

ITALY

TEMPEH

INDONESIA

EZ-MELTER

SOUTH AMERICA

DUMPLINGS

POLAND

FOODIE ADVENTURES

People often ask me what diet I follow when I travel and I respond by asking what planet they're from. It only seems fair. The words 'travel' and 'diet' should never under any circumstances fall within the same sentence.

Being in a new place is about embracing the unknown. Everything around you is different – the people, the culture, the FOOD! Travelling is about opening yourself up to all of these things, trying new things and, of course, tasting new things!

However, being genetically blessed with a fast metabolism that burns through endless pizzas, gelato and carb-heavy pastas is not something we are all given as a birthright. So I present to you:

The No-Diet Travel Diet
(because no one should say no to crème brûlée in the French capital)

It's pretty simple.

- **Try everything.** Don't say no to anything and for the life of you, don't ask if there is a 'light' version. Have a small taste of the dish exactly as it is presented to you.

- **Avoid deep-fried.** Just because you want to try everything doesn't mean you need to have a whole large frites to yourself every other travel day.

- **Limit sugar.** While it's fine to obey the first golden rule to try everything, that doesn't mean you must try everything thrice. Limit your sugar intake and spoil yourself once per day.

- **High protein, moderate carbohydrates, good fats.** These are the core considerations when choosing a meal at a restaurant.

- **Drink plenty of water.**

TRAVEL BEAUTY PRODUCTS THAT WILL CHANGE YOUR LIFE

There are some beauty products I swear by, some I can't live without, and then there's my travel supply: the bare necessities in travel-friendly containers and cases. Some of these products are genius, others magic, and here's why you should know about all of them (seriously, we're talking life-changing here).

Perfume in a travel tube

The geniuses over at Le Labo have solved the dilemma of smelling great while travelling without the risk of expensive perfume breaking in transit and spilling through your luggage. This screw-top metal travel tube will ensure no spillage and believe me when I say these scents are to die for!

Dry shampoo

Dry shampoo is just what it sounds like: shampoo in a dry form that is sprayed onto dirty hair to rough it up and put shape back into it. When your hair begins to feel oily, naturally you would choose to wash it to cleanse it from the nasties and replenish it with essential oils. While dry shampoo doesn't wash your hair for you (now that really would be magic), it does delay the need to wash your hair for a few more days.

Root concealer

Root concealer has been a lifesaver for me – sold in a can, this is what I would describe as 'spray painting your roots' so they blend with the rest of your hair colour. Specifically for concealing roots, it's safe and it works a treat!

Nail-polish wipes

Forget the days of worrying about spillage in your suitcase! Nail-polish wipes are the answer to being able to paint your nails on holiday and remove or change the colour as much as you please, without the hassle of carrying around bulky nail-polish remover.

Compressed towels

Some things really are just magic. Compressed towels are about the size of a small coin but once placed in water, they expand to the size of a face washer. With a few of these in your hand luggage you're sure to always feel cleansed and refreshed!

BB cream with SPF

After years and years of swearing by foundation as my one 'must have' makeup item, my introduction to BB quickly put those days behind me. BB cream acts as something between a tinted moisturiser and a foundation, adjusting to your skin tone and resulting in an even glow. Be sure to find a brand with SPF 30+ included, as this will give you both gorgeous skin and sun protection – all in one quick face rub in the morning!

Nail files

Nail files are nothing new to the scene but they are handy weapons to have in your makeup kit when travelling. There's nothing worse than breaking a nail and not being able to tame it so it doesn't catch on anything and everything!

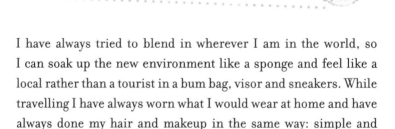

TRAVEL MAKEUP

(in under two minutes)

I have always tried to blend in wherever I am in the world, so I can soak up the new environment like a sponge and feel like a local rather than a tourist in a bum bag, visor and sneakers. While travelling I have always worn what I would wear at home and have always done my hair and makeup in the same way: simple and whatever works that day.

But I do have a ritual I follow every morning – what I'd like to call two-minute travel makeup. It's simple and straight to the point. It will leave you feeling fresh-faced without having to worry if your foundation will melt in the sun and run all the way down past your armpits.

- At the risk of stating the obvious, it is an absolute necessity to cleanse your face every morning before you start the day and every evening before you finish the day. While you might think this is a waste of time when you travel, your skin will thank you later and you won't require any additional makeup (like concealer or heavy powders) because you won't have any blemishes that need covering up! Clear skin is your best asset and better than the magic of any makeup.

- Moisturising is another obvious must-do to keep your skin hydrated, especially when you travel, as air-conditioning systems will dry out your skin and leave it feeling lifeless.

- BB cream is a life-saving angel sent from the heavens above. There truly is no other product that is as essential in a traveller's product bag! BB cream provides light coverage, so when combined with a little foundation for long-lasting results you really can't go wrong. Be sure to pick a brand with SPF included to keep your skin protected from the sun.

- Illuminator is my secret weapon when travelling. It has a way of instantly making you look wide awake and fresh-faced, even when you've just stepped off a fourteen-hour flight. Apply it to your upper cheekbones and add a slight dab on your upper lip and nose line to highlight your complexion.

- Last but never least, mascara. The original and the best combatant against appearing jet-lagged.

HOW TO TAKE BETTER
TRAVEL PHOTOS

Once upon a time I was a point-and-shoot kinda girl. I would see something I wanted to remember, rush to grab my camera from my backpack, point my camera towards the subject, shoot, and be done.

Needless to say I didn't capture any groundbreaking travel photos that way.

My photos have certainly come a long way since those days. I am now more creative and more interested in the subjects I am photographing. Everything I capture is a piece in my jigsaw, a step in my journey and a reminder of the people I've met, the places I've been, and of the stories I want to tell for years to come.

Over the years I've learned a lot of little things that have helped me capture better travel photos. While I still have a long way to go, all of my advice is easy to apply, in real talk (no fancy terms), and will help amateurs and enthusiasts capture their travels in a way that makes them worthy of a frame on the mantelpiece.

Before you go, plan

Travel photography starts before you've even walked out your front door. In order to capture great photos and great stories, you need to think about what you're capturing.

- Research your destination.
- Find locations you wish to photograph and make a list before you go.
- Use Pinterest to visually research each place.
- Create scenes in your head and consider any props you might need.
- Map it out.
- Make it happen!

Before you shoot, think

When you arrive at your destination, be sure to take a minute to consider what is going on around you. Before you take a hundred photos of the Eiffel Tower, consider the people around you and how they will look. Better to capture a lovely old couple admiring the tower than a tonne of tourists huddled in a big group for their own snapshot!

- Be patient and wait for people to move.
- Look for different angles and perspectives.
- Look for ways to tell a story rather than just photographing the subject itself.
- Consider your surroundings.

Composition

The way you compose your photo is the determining factor
between a good and a great photo. By traditional wisdom,
you should avoid the centre and apply the 'rule of thirds'
when taking photos . . . but rules were made to be broken!

So, what is the rule of thirds?

• This theory is (almost) as old as time, concluding that a
photograph should be split into nine equal parts and the focal
point of the image should fall into place where any two lines cross.
This results in the focal point being in a third of the image,
making for an aesthetically pleasing shot – but should it
be considered as a rule or, rather, a guideline?

• Don't be afraid of the centre. When photographing
a powerful subject (i.e. a striking building of symmetrical
proportions or a portrait), positioning the subject in
the middle can often lead to great results.

• The rule of thirds is good to follow when trying to photograph
a person in the frame with an impressive landscape.

• Don't be afraid to use the foreground when shooting
landscape photos, as this often tells a better story
and puts things into perspective.

• Know when to take photos up close (i.e. when photographing
details of a building, portraits, flora and fauna), yet also
know when to take a step back.

Angles

One of the easiest ways to make your travel photos stand out is by doing things differently. If everyone has a photo of the Louvre Pyramid from straight on with the subject in the centre, what is going to make your photo different and better?

- Get low, get high, move around.

- Find alternative perspectives, like a balcony or from behind a column.

- Let the angles tell a story. For example harsh lines create a striking image, whereas whimsical grass waving blurrily in the foreground of a photo will result in a dreamy setting for the backdrop.

Lighting

Lighting is a vital consideration in determining how your photo will turn out.

- Natural light is always best.

- Golden hour, with its gorgeous warm tones, is the hour before sunset and is great for capturing images.

- Avoid shooting in the middle of the day when the light can be harsh.

- Worried about the weather being overcast? Fear not! These are great conditions for photography.

- Don't be afraid to edit photos in post-production if the lighting was not working in your favour or you're still learning. Practice makes perfect!

People

People are often the best way to share the story of a new destination, they will help you capture the personality and life behind a city or place.

- Photographing people up close is an invasion of their privacy, so be sure to ask first and have some coins in your pockets to offer as money is often requested in return for taking a photograph.

- Photographing people from long distances without detailing their face is fine. However, it often misses the detail in sharing the story behind the face.

- When photographing people, be sure to take the time to thank them and perhaps even speak with them to learn more about their life and culture. The photo is just the beginning – the story is what wins people's hearts.

Landscapes

Landscapes are often the most popular photos to take on your travels, in order to showcase the impressive views of a city, coastlines, fields of tulips, etc. Follow these simple tips to improve your landscape photography:

- Shoot landscapes at golden hour for the best light.

- Shoot early in the morning before crowds form and a city wakes up.

- Avoid shooting in the middle of the day to avoid harsh light.

- Investing in a wide-angle lens will allow you to fit more into your photo.

- A tripod is essential when photographing in low light. Consider investing in a small travel-friendly tripod to capture these moments too.

POST-TRAVEL
DETOX

In the world we live in today, there are so many crazy diets and fitness regimes being offered up to us that it is often hard to know what is right and what is wrong. The safest bet is to lead an ongoing healthy lifestyle – to eat well, get enough sleep, drink plenty of water, and to maintain fitness, even if that just means walking more.

I have a ten-day post-travel detox that is simple, effective, and that refreshes my body after any overindlugences enjoyed abroad.

Ten-day Detox

(That won't leave you hungry or angry)

Rather than sticking to a strict regimen, there are just a few simple rules to remember when detoxing from a big trip.

- Only eat when you're hungry.

- Drink plenty of water – a minimum of six glasses per day.

- Drink unlimited herbal tea (but no coffee, juice or cordials).

- Eat a big breakfast with no refined sugars. This could include toast, eggs or smoothies.

- Snack throughout the day avoiding only sugar, deep-fried food and packaged food. Eat fresh wherever possible.

- Eat the rainbow at dinner – a large variety of vegetables goes a long way.

- Don't forbid yourself a light dessert if you are craving something and need a reward for your day of healthy eating.

- Always finish with a peppermint herbal tea before bed.

The most important thing to remember is that each of us is different and our bodies all have different needs. Listen to your body and act accordingly. Make your own set of rules that will suit your body and your needs for a healthy detox. Remember never to starve your body of the nutrients it needs as this will result in more harm than good!

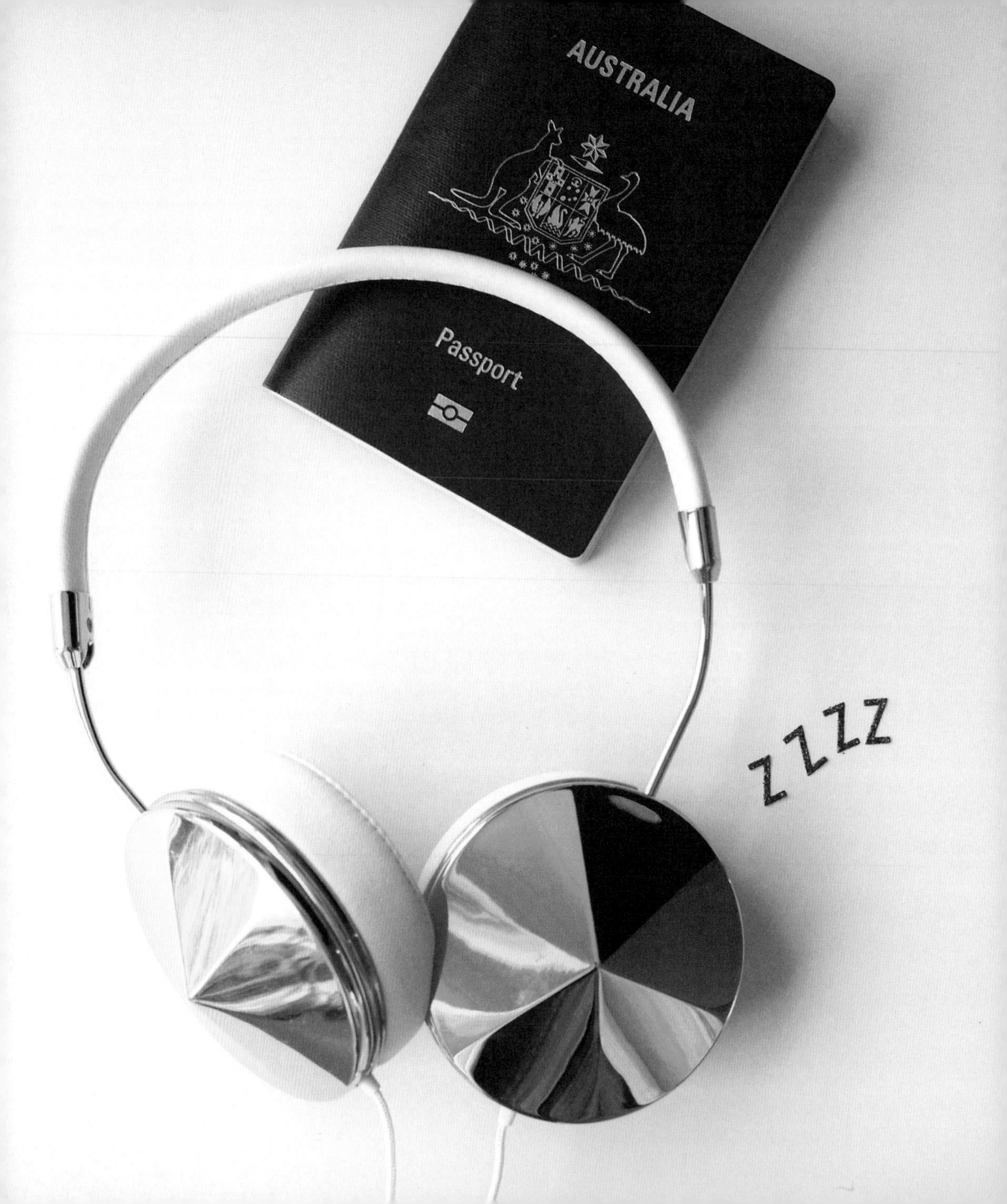
AUSTRALIA
Passport
ZZZZ

HOW TO BEAT JETLAG

Yes, there are tried-and-tested ways to combat jetlag. Yes, they actually work. Here's how to combat jetlag and shake it as soon as you land.

No alcohol but plenty of water.

No coffee, tea or caffeinated drinks (stimulants are out).

Don't sleep during the day; adjust immediately
to your new time zone.

Spend your arrival day outdoors in the sunshine and fresh air.

Take a shower or go for a swim, it truly feels like liquid sleep!

Go to bed between 8 and 10 p.m. in your new time zone –
not too early but not too late.

Wake up feeling refreshed,
and seize the day!

THE ULTIMATE
ADVENTURES MEMOIR

Making an adventures memoir is one of the best ways to look back at your travels and create something from those memories. So head to your local craft store, stock up on beautiful papers, stickers, glitter and anything else you fancy and let's get to work!

What you'll need:

- Plain A5 binder
- Travel memories – photographs, postcards, tickets, menus, business cards, polaroids, anything memorable!
- Hole punch
- A5 plastic sleeves
- Glue stick
- Craft supplies: stickers, colourful paper, patterned paper, etc.

Planning it out:

- Before using glue, visualise your ideas and piece them together to ensure you can change your mind if necessary!
- When on an adventure, keep lots of momentos like receipts, business cards or a dry leaf if you so wish.
- Remember to capture everything in different ways: food up close, landscapes far away, photograph your feet, face away from the camera and don't be afraid to try new things!
- When piecing together your album, be sure to write cute little notes to remind you of something that was said that day, or a person you met and why they intrigued you. These are the memories you will want to hold onto forever.
- Never plan to finish – this is a book that should carry on (albeit in multiple volumes if you travel a lot) throughout your lifetime.

WHAT TO DO WITH YOUR PHOTOS – 4 DIFFERENT WAYS

There's one souvenir that trumps all others and that is travel photos. But so often these days they stay in digital form where nobody will ever see them. Here are a few fun ideas for what to do with your travel photos to let the memories last a lifetime!

1. Hang on a String

This is one of the simplest ways to reminisce about your latest adventure – plus you can always change the photos with each trip you take!

3. Tile over a Wall

If you're one of those people who needs adventure like they need oxygen, then the best way to make it through the day in between trips is to carry on reminiscing (while you plan the next one)! Have your photos printed to the same size for a neat, tiled effect, or use all different shapes and sizes to emphasise the trips and moments you love the most.

2. Make a Photo Book

If your photos are in digital form, you can still have them printed to create a gorgeous coffee-table book with a professional finish. Many printing companies offer this service online and it can be a great conversation starter when friends are visiting.

4. Make a Travel Scrapbook

Travel scrapbooks are a fun way to relive your adventures and create a long-lasting personalised memory book. This is a great activity for a rainy day when you have the post-travel blues.

CORKBOARD MAP

One of my favourite pieces of art in my house is my DIY corkboard map. It's really simple and easy to do and the fact that you have made it yourself makes it all the more special! It is my constant reminder that no matter how far I have travelled, there's still a long way to go.

What you'll need:

- Poster map (A1 size)
- Corkboard (cut to 59.4 cm x 84.1cm)
- Frame (A1 size) without glass
- PVA glue
- Water
- Paintbrush
- Pins

Method:

- Purchase a map that you would like to use for the project. If you can't find an antique or sepia map and would like to convert a coloured map, simply pour black coffee or tea over the coloured map and allow it to dry in the sun. Continue this process a couple of times until you have the desired shade.

- Mix a cup of PVA glue with ⅓ cup of water, using a paintbrush to mix together.

- With your paintbrush, cover the corkboard in a layer of glue and allow to dry a little so that it is sticky to touch.

- Then place your map on top of the glue and firmly press down. If you have used coffee or tea to age your map, you may find a bubble effect in the map when gluing it down – but don't worry, it just adds to the effect!

- Now put two layers of glue over top of the poster, allowing it to dry between coats.

- Frame your map.

- Now it's time to start pinning!

HOW TO
ESCAPE

(without actually going anywhere)

TRAVEL NEAR AND FAR

Sometimes you just need to get away, like, five minutes ago. If you feel the urge for a spontaneous adventure, here are a few quick getaway ideas that won't require a passport.

Watch a sunset

Sometimes, more than needing to go somewhere, we need to escape reality and focus our energies on something else. Taking a moment to enjoy a sunset – to stop, breathe, and be thankful – will feel like an escape in itself.

Go to the ocean

There's no place I feel more connected to the rest of the world than by the ocean. No matter where you are, somewhere on the other side of your ocean someone is feeling the exact same way.

Go for a run

With our modern lifestyles it often feels impossible to disconnect from everything around us and reconnect with ourselves. Running has a way of clearing your mind, as you just focus on putting one foot in front of the other, and is a great way to escape without actually going anywhere (except for the round-trip of your run, of course!).

Yoga

At its core, yoga is the union between your mind, body and soul. So while the health benefits of yoga include flexibility and muscle strength, they also extend to mental benefits. If you need an escape into your inner self, consider a yoga class – you won't know until you've tried!

Build a cubbyhouse in your living room

Always remember that nothing is gained by taking life too seriously. As kids we barely take anything seriously but as adults we somehow find ourselves doing the exact opposite. When it's just 'one of those days', build a fort, bury yourself in it, and live your cubbyhouse fantasy with a pillow, a blanket, a torch and a good book (sustenance is good, too!)

DAY TRIP ADVENTURES

As travel between borders becomes more and more accessible, we often overlook the opportunities that are closest to home. It is important to remember that no matter where you are in the world, someone somewhere wants to be right where you are. Until teleportation arrives, here are some great day adventures to ease your restless feet:

Pack a picnic.

Swim by a waterfall.

Go for a bike ride.

Enjoy a day hike.

Grab your friends and go to a tourist
hot spot you've never been to before.

HOW TO HAVE A
Mexican Fiesta!

23 Oct. 2006
CURVA1
695

For those times you just want to get away to foreign lands
and surround yourself with the sea, sand and sun, you've got
to let your imagination run wild and bring the party to you!

Step one: set the scene

The best way to transport yourself
(and your party guests) far, far away
is to get every inch of the detail right.
When hosting a Mexican fiesta, it is
essential to let colour fill your room.
This means reds, yellows, pinks, greens,
blues and every other shade of the
rainbow. Go all out and set the scene
with the works: flowers, colourful plates,
napkins and candles, and the
all important centrepiece, the piñata.

Step two: the arrival

For the arrival, be sure to greet your
guests with tortilla chips and guacamole,
plus a powerful sorbet margarita or
colourful lemonade for the little ones.
Garnishes are a must and this is one
time those colourful drink umbrellas
are not just acceptable – they're
a necessity.

Step three: starters

The Mexican fiesta is all about the food: lots and lots of food.
Be sure to offer a variety for each course, as the Mexican
fiesta is also about sharing and trying little bits of everything.
Some good starter ideas include quesadillas, chilled soups and,
of course, more guacamole!

Step four: main course

Nothing beats a help-yourself taco and burrito bar. That being said, providing loads of options is the absolute key to success. Prior to the guests arriving, be sure to prepare an assortment of choices such as cheese, lettuce, tomato, onion, mixed salad, beans, sour cream and guacamole. For the filling you'll need a couple of meat varieties and a veggie option to be on the safe side.
Then let the feast begin!

Step five: desserts, drinks and the all-important piñata!

Be sure to prepare plenty of drinks to keep your guests topped up throughout the night, as well as keeping plenty of ice on hand for those too-easy-to-drink-margaritas! Keep your dessert fresh, simple and fun: something fruity with a hint of chocolate or, if you want to really impress your guests, you can't go past a generous serving of churros with warm chocolate dipping sauce. Then, to conclude the night, let the kids (and adults) go wild with a game of piñata!

RECREATING THE MAGIC OF GERMAN CHRISTMAS MARKETS AT HOME

The traditional Christmas markets in Europe will undoubtedly steal your heart. The atmosphere is unlike anything else and, despite the cold temperature, the food, wine and people will warmly welcome you. To recreate the magic of the Christmas markets at home you'll need:

Christmas lights

Christmas music

Mulled wine (glühwein)

Gingerbread hearts

Candied almonds

Roasted chestnuts

Gift giving

HOSTING A BRITISH HIGH TEA

Place sweets and savouries on platters or tiered serving trays.
As this is a proper British affair, be sure to keep sweets and
savouries separate, and make everything bite sized. Include
bite-sized sandwiches, scones, patisseries and cakes.

Do not forget to dress your table with serviettes.

Scones are a necessity. Serve them warm and with small pots
of jam and clotted cream for your guests to enjoy.

Now for the tea. Opt for loose-leaf tea if you're trying to
impress your guests, or else tea bags will do just fine. Whatever
the case, have a selection of teas on offer so your guests feel
spoiled for choice. Coffee is most certainly not to be served.

Sugar and milk must be readily available for your guests
to add at their own leisure. These should be placed in
an obvious and accessible location on the table.

If entertaining in hot weather, iced tea makes
for a great summer alternative.

Pinkies up!

Best Travel Movies to Cure Your Wanderlust

The Beach
(2000)

Out of Africa
(1985)

Lost in Translation
(2003)

The Secret Life of Walter Mitty
(2013)

Into the Wild
(2007)

Under the Tuscan Sun
(2003)

The Motorcycle Diaries
(2004)

The Sisterhood of the Traveling Pants
(2005)

In Bruges
(2008)

The Endless Summer
(1966)

HOW TO MAKE THE
MOST OUT OF LIFE

Travel to all seven continents

Learn a new language

Move to a new city in a new country

Start your own business

Learn yoga and reach an advanced level

Run a marathon

Volunteer for a cause that matters to you

Ride horseback

Join a team for a sport you've
never played before

Climb a mountain

Give without expectation of receiving

Pursue your passions . . . all of them

Fly in a hot air balloon

Secretly pay for the next person
in line behind you

Dance in the rain

See as many sunrises and
sunsets as you can

Live within your means

Spend more time outdoors

Instead of giving money, give time.
There is nothing more valuable

Know that fear is the thief of joy.
You can achieve anything you
set your mind to

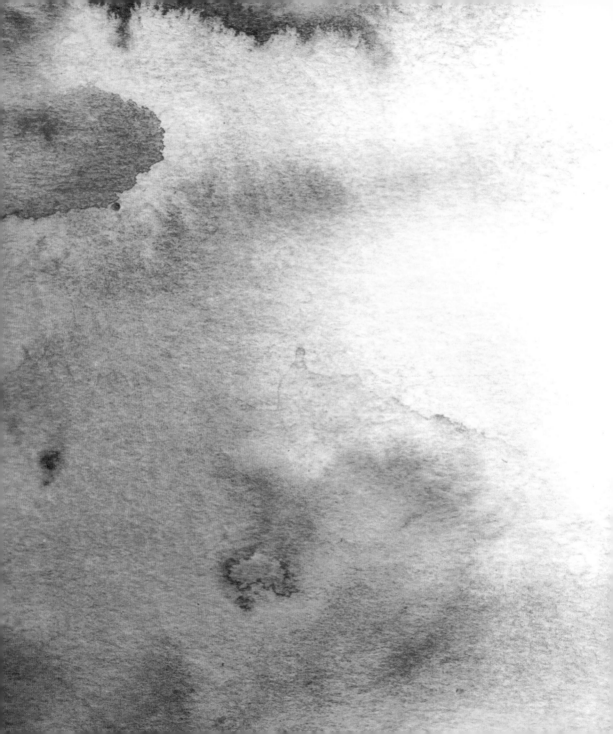

WANDERLUST
DIRECTORY

wanderlust top ten

HOTELS

SINGITA SWENI
Kruger National Park, South Africa
singita.com/sweni-lodge

ELLERMAN HOUSE
Cape Town, South Africa
ellerman.co.za

NIHIWATU RESORT
Sumba Island, Indonesia
nihiwatu.com

CASA DEL MAR
Santa Monica, USA
hotelcasadelmar.com

ALILA VILLAS ULUWATU
Bali, Indonesia
alilahotels.com/uluwatu

THE PIERRE, A TAJ HOTEL
New York, USA
tajhotels.com

ROYAL DAVUI
Mbengga, Fiji
royaldavuifiji.com

LE TOINY
Toiny, St Barthelemy
letoiny.com

ROYAL MANSOUR
Marrakech, Morocco
royalmansour.com

THE RITZ CARLTON HOTEL
Hong Kong, China
ritzcarlton.com

wanderlust top ten

RESTAURANTS

LE CINQ, PARIS
31 Avenue George V, Paris, France

restaurant-lecinq.com

LA VETTA, AROSA
Tschuggen Grand Hotel,
Arosa, Switzerland

tschuggen.ch

WARUNG, BALI
Alila Villas, Uluwatu, Bali, Indonesia

alilahotels.com

LES LABOURS, BAIE-SAINT-PAUL
Hotel Le Germain Charlevoix,
Baie-Saint-Paul, Canada

legermainhotels.com

STILLWATER, AUSTRALIA
2 Bridge Road, Launceston, Tasmania, Australia

stillwater.com.au

DELAIRE GRAFF RESTAURANT SOUTH AFRICA
Delaire Graff Estate, Helshoogte Pass,
Stellenbosch, South Africa

delaire.co.za

MOM TRI'S KITCHEN, THAILAND
12 Kata Noi Road, Phuket, Thailand

villaroyalephuket.com

TIM HO WAN, HONG KONG
18 Hoi Ting Road, Hong Kong

timhowan.com

GASTROLOGIK, SWEDEN
Artillerigatan 14, Stockholm, Sweden

gastrologik.se

THE BAZAAR BY JOSÉ ANDRÉS, USA
S La Cienega Blvd, Los Angeles,
CA, USA

sbe.com

wanderlust top ten

BARS

ARTESIAN, LONDON
1C Portland Place, London, UK
Artesian-bar.co.uk

DEAD RABBIT, NEW YORK
30 Water Street, New York, USA
Deadrabbitnyc.com

**28 HONG KONG STREET,
SINGAPORE**
28 Hong Kong Street, Singapore
28hks.com

CANDELARIA, PARIS
52 Rue de Saintongue, Paris, France
Candelariaparis.com

ATTABOY, NEW YORK
134 Eldridge Street, New York, USA

BUCK & BRECK, BERLIN
Brunnenstraße 177, Berlin, Germany
Buckandbreck.com

DELICATESSEN, MOSCOW
Sadovaya-Karetnaya ul. 20, Moscow,
Russia
A-a-ah.com/delicatessen

BLACK PEARL, MELBOURNE
304 Brunswick Street, Fitzroy, Australia
Blackpearlbar.com.au

RUBY, COPENHAGEN
Nybrogade 10, 1203 Copenhagen,
Denmark
Rby.dk

ZUMA DUBAI, DUBAI
Dubai Financial Centre, UAE
Zumarestaurant.com

wanderlust top ten

COFFEE SHOPS & TEA HOUSES

CAFÉ SPERL, VIENNA
Gumpendorfer Str. 11, Vienna, Austria
cafesperl.at

ANGELINA, PARIS
226 Rue de Rivoli, Paris, France
angelina-paris.fr

BLACKBIRD TEA ROOM, BRIGHTON
30 Ship Street, Brighton, UK
blackbirdtearooms.com

CLARIDGE'S, LONDON
Brook Street, London, UK
claridges.co.uk

LUCY'S TEAROOM, THE COTSWOLDS
The Square, Stow-on-the-Wold,
Cheltenham, Gloucestershire, UK

RAFFLES HOTEL, SINGAPORE
1 Beach Road, Singapore
raffles.com

TOP PADDOCK, MELBOURNE
658 Church Street, Richmond, Australia
toppaddockcafe.com

ROSATI, ROME
Piazza del Popolo, 5a, Rome, Italy
barrosati.com

**BROOKLYN ROASTING COMPANY,
NEW YORK**
25 Jay Street, Brooklyn, USA
brooklynroasting.com

HARDWARE SOCIETE, MELBOURNE
120 Hardware Street, Melbourne, Australia

THEATRES

**PALAIS GARNIER,
PARIS, FRANCE**

operadeparis.fr

**SHAKESPEARE'S GLOBE,
LONDON, UK**

shakespearesglobe.com

**BOLSHOI THEATRE,
MOSCOW, RUSSIA**

bolshoi.ru

**SYDNEY OPERA HOUSE,
SYDNEY, AUSTRALIA**

sydneyoperahouse.com

**VIENNA STATE OPERA,
VIENNA, AUSTRIA**

wiener-staatsoper.at

**ROYAL OPERA HOUSE,
LONDON, UK**

roh.org.uk

**RADIO CITY MUSIC HALL,
NEW YORK, USA**

radiocity.com

**MARIINSKY THEATRE,
ST PETERSBURG, RUSSIA**

mariinsky.ru

**METROPOLITAN OPERA HOUSE,
NEW YORK CITY, USA**

metopera.org

**TEATRO ALLA SCALA,
MILAN, ITALY**

teatroallascalla.org

wanderlust top ten

MUSEUMS

THE HERMITAGE, ST PETERSBURG
Palace Square, 2, St Petersburg, Russia
hermitagemuseum.com

**METROPOLITAN MUSEUM OF ART,
NEW YORK**
1000 5th Ave, New York, USA
metmuseum.org

MUSÉE D'ORSAY, PARIS
1 Rue de la Légion d'Honneur, Paris, France
musee-orsay.fr

THE LOUVRE, PARIS
75001 Paris, France
louvre.fr

RIJKSMUSEUM, AMSTERDAM
Museumstraat 1, Amsterdam, Netherlands
rijksmuseum.nl

**SMITHSONIAN INSTITUTION,
WASHINGTON DC, USA**
Locations throughout central DC, USA
si.edu

BRITISH MUSEUM, LONDON
Great Russell Street, London, UK
britishmuseum.org

MUSEUM OF MODERN ART
11 W 53rd Street, New York, USA
moma.org

TATE MODERN, LONDON
Bankside, London, UK
tate.org.uk

**VICTORIA & ALBERT MUSEUM,
LONDON**
Cromwell Road, London, UK
vam.ac.uk

Acknowledgements

What a journey it has been to see my travels come to life on
these pages! I would first and foremost love to thank God,
my family and my supportive friends. I would also like to
send a big thank you to my biggest fan and confidante,
my partner William. And an even bigger (the biggest)
thank you to my dedicated blog readers. You have been
with me from the beginning of this journey and
my heart is forever full o' love for you all!

love, Brooke xo

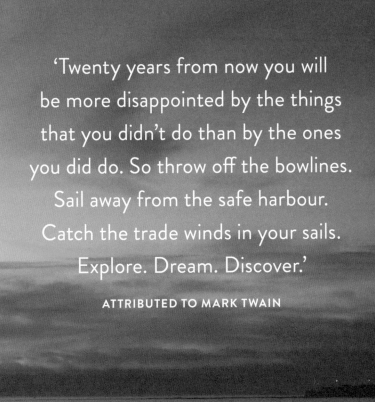

'Twenty years from now you will
be more disappointed by the things
that you didn't do than by the ones
you did do. So throw off the bowlines.
Sail away from the safe harbour.
Catch the trade winds in your sails.
Explore. Dream. Discover.'

ATTRIBUTED TO MARK TWAIN

VIKING

UK | USA | Canada | Ireland | Australia
India | New Zealand | South Africa | China

Penguin Books is part of the Penguin Random House group of companies
whose addresses can be found at global.penguinrandomhouse.com.

Penguin
Random House
Australia

First published by Penguin Group (Australia), 2016

1 3 5 7 9 10 8 6 4 2

Text copyright © Brooke Saward, 2016.

The moral right of the author has been asserted.

All rights reserved. Without limiting the rights under copyright reserved above,
no part of this publication may be reproduced, stored in or introduced into
a retrieval system, or transmitted, in any form or by any means (electronic,
mechanical, photocopying, recording or otherwise), without the prior written
permission of both the copyright owner and the above publisher of this book.

Cover design by Adam Laszczuk © Penguin Group (Australia)
Text design by Laura Thomas © Penguin Group (Australia)
Cover photograph by Brooke Saward
Photography by Brooke Saward;
photographs on p. 76-77, 78, 82, 85, 90, 91 by Faye Bullock;
photographs on p. 24, 157, 187, 210, 212-213 by Emma Kate Codrington
Internal illustrations by Grace West
Colour separation by Splitting Image Colour Studio, Clayton, Victoria
Printed and bound in China by RR Donnelley Asia Printing Solutions Limited.

National Library of Australia Cataloguing-in-publication data is available.

ISBN: 978 0 670 07932 2

penguin.com.au